MW01709487

THE GREAT SEAFOOD COOKBOOK

R&R PUBLICATIONS MARKETING PTY LTD

Published by
R&R Publications Marketing Pty. Ltd.
ACN 27 083 612 579
12 Edward Street, Brunswick, Victoria, 3056
Australia wide toll free: 1800 063 296

The Great Seafood Cookbook

Publisher: Richard Carroll
Production Manager: Anthony Carroll
Creative Director: Frank Turco
Cover Design: Karl Roper
Food Photography: Warren Webb, Andrew Elton
Food for Photography: Olivier Massart, Jenny Fenshaw, Kazu Takahashi
Food Stylist: Di Kirby, Stephanie Souvlis
Recipe Development: Ellen Argyriou, Olivier Massart, Jenny Fenshaw,
Stephanie Souvlis, Masakazu Hori, Tamara Milstein (12, 22, 80, 174, 212)
Proof Reader: Fiona Brodribb

The National Library of Australia
Cataloguing-in-Publication Data
The Great Seafood Cookbook
Includes Index
ISBN 1 74022 174 5
1. Cookery (Seafood)
641 692

First Edition Printed August 2002
Typeset in Verdana, Triplex, Helvetica and Avenir

Printed in Singapore

contents

buying and storing fish

When buying fish for your family and friends, make sure it is fresh, and if you plan to freeze it, don't buy fish that has already been frozen. There are a few things to look for to tell if fish is fresh:

- It should not have a strong odour. Instead it should have a pleasant and mild 'sea' smell.
- The flesh should be firm with a smooth, slippery skin and no yellow discolouration.
- Whole fish should have bright eyes and red gills.

If you are worried about children swallowing bones, look for the many cuts available without bones. Try flake (also boneless hake), swordfish, marlin, tuna, blue grenadier, sea perch, salmon, John Dory, tail-pieces of ocean trout, ling and blue-eye cod . You will also find that many fish-mongers now sell de-boned fillets such as salmon and trout.

If the fish has been packed in a plastic bag, unwrap it as soon as you get home and place it in a glass or stainless steel dish.

Cover lightly with a damp tea towel and keep in the coolest part of the refrigerator.

Use as soon as possible, and if not using the next day, place over a pan of ice.

If freezing, wrap fillets individually in plastic cling wrap for easy separation. Always defrost in the fridge or microwave, or cook from frozen. Never thaw at room temperature, and never refreeze thawed fish.

Pic 1

Pic 2

Pic 3

Pic 4

Pic 5

Pic 6

Preparing Fish

The two types of fish discussed here are described as flatfish (eg flouder and sole) and roundfish (eg snapper, cod). Both types need to be cleaned before use, but cleaning procedures vary.

SCALING AND FINNING

Most fish will need to be scaled. However, there are a few exceptions, such as trout, tuna, shark, leatherjacket and others described in this book.

When poaching a whole unboned fish, it is best to leave the dorsal and anal fins attached. This will to help hold the fish together during cooking. Rinse fish.

Wash fish and leave wet as a wet fish is easier to scale. Remove scales using a knife or scaler and start at the tail and scrape towards the head. (Pic 1)

Clip the dorsal fin with scissors or, if desired, remove both the dorsal and anal fins by cutting along the side of the fin with a sharp knife. Then pull the fin towards the head to remove it.
(Pic 2)

GUTTING

Gutting techniques are different for roundfish and flatfish. When preparing fish to bone or fillet, remove the entrails by gutting through the belly. If you wish to serve the fish whole, preserve the shape of the fish by gutting through the gills.

Roundfish

For boning or filleting, cut off the head behind gill opening. Use a sharp knife and cut open belly from head to just above anal fin. Remove membranes, veins and viscera. Rinse thoroughly. (Pic 3)

To preserve shape of round fish, cut through the gills and open outer gill with the thumb. Put a finger into the gill and snag the inner gill. Gently pull to remove inner gill and viscera. Rinse well. (Pic 4)

Flatfish

To gut, make a small cut behind gills and pull out viscera. (Pic 5)

SKINNING

The tasty skin of some fish enhances the flavour. However, other fish have strong or inedible skin that interferes with the flavour. Always leave skin on when poaching or grilling a whole fish.

Round fish

When skinning a whole round fish, make a slit across the body behind the gills, with another just above the tail. Then make another cut down the back. (Pic 6)

Pic 7

Pic 8

Pic 9

Pic 10

Pic 11

Pic 12

Using a sharp knife, start at the tail and separate the skin from the flesh. Pull the knife towards the head, whilst holding the skin firmly with the other hand. Do not 'saw' the knife. (Pic 7)

Flatfish

Skin a whole flatfish, by first turning the dark side up, then cutting across the skin where the tail joins the body. With a sharp knife, peel the skin back towards the head until you have enough skin to hold with one hand. (Pic 8)

Anchor the fish with one hand and pull the skin over the head. Turn fish over and hold the head while pulling the skin down to the tail. (Pic 9)

CUTTING FILLETS

Fillets are pieces of boneless fish. There are slightly different techniques for filleting roundfish and flatfish.

Roundfish

With a sharp knife, make a slit along the backbone from head to tail, then make a cut behind the gill.

Hold the head and insert the knife between fillet and ribs. Slide knife along the ribs (do not use a sawing motion), and cut down the length of the fish. Remove fillet by cutting off at the anal fin. Repeat on the other side of fish.

Flatfish

Place skinned fish on chopping board with eyes up. Cut from head to tail through the flesh in the middle of the fish to the backbone. Insert a sharp knife between the ribs and the end of the fillet near the head. Pull knife down the fillet on one side of the backbone and remove. (Pic 10)

Cut off the remaining fillet in the same manner. Turn fish over and remove the two bottom fillets. (Pic 11)

SKINNING A FILLET

Place fillet skin side down and cut a small piece of flesh away from the skin close to the tail. Hold skin tight, and run a sharp knife along the skin without cutting it. (Pic 12)

CUTTING A STEAK OR CUTLET

Using a solid, sharp chef's knife, cut off head just behind the gills. Slice the fish into steaks or cutlets of the desired thickness. (Pic 13)

Pic 14

Pic 15

Pic 16

Pic 17

Pic 18

Preparing Shellfish

preparation

A diverse and astonishing variety of univalves (abalone), bivalves (oysters, clams and mussels), crustaceans (crabs, prawns and lobsters) and cephalopods (squid and octopus) is available for our cooking pot. However, there is one point of concern: out of water, shellfish deteriorate quickly.

OPENING BIVALVES

All bivalves – oysters, clams and mussels – should be tightly closed when purchased.

If you wish to use the shells in cooking, scrub them with a stiff brush under cold, running water.

Oysters

If you use technique rather than strength, oysters are easy to open. Hold the unopened oyster in a garden glove or tea towel (which will protect one hand from the rough shell) while you open the shell with an oyster knife, held in the other hand.

Hold the oyster with the deep cut down. Insert the tip of the oyster knife into the hinge, then twist to open the shell. Do not open oyster by attempting to insert the oyster knife into the front lip of the shell. (Pic 14)

Slide the oyster knife inside the upper shell to cut the muscle that attaches oyster to the shell. To serve, discard the upper part of shell and cut muscle under bottom half, then re-place oyster into half-shell. (Pic 15)

Clams

To open clams, use a blunt clam-knife to avoid cutting the meat. Try freezing bivalves for half an hour to relax the muscles – they will be easier to open.

Slide blade of clam-knife between two halves of shell. Work knife towards hinge until shell parts. (Pic 16)

Slide blade along inside of one shell to cut muscles. Then do the same to other side to dislodge flesh. (Pic 17)

Mussels

The threads of tissue that protrude from the mussel shell are called the byssus or, more commonly, the beard. As mussels die quickly after debearding, prepare them immediately. Use the same technique for opening as for clams. (Pic 18)

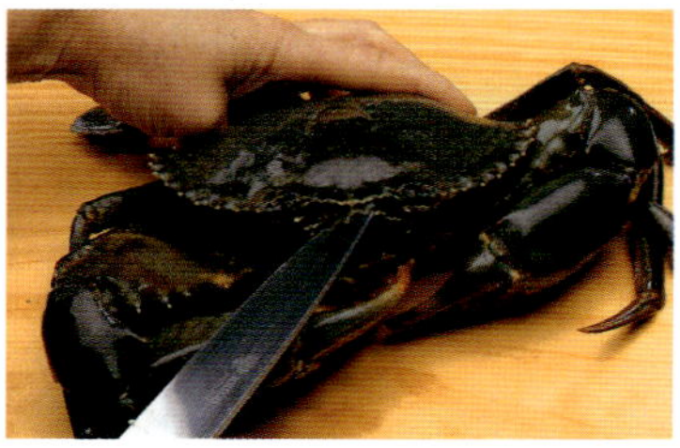

Pic 19

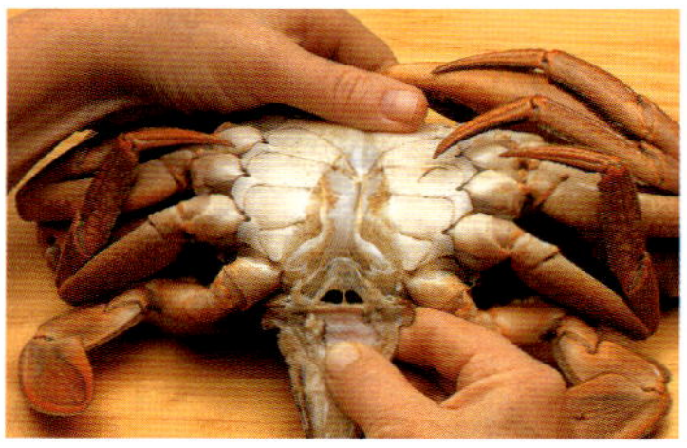

Pic 20

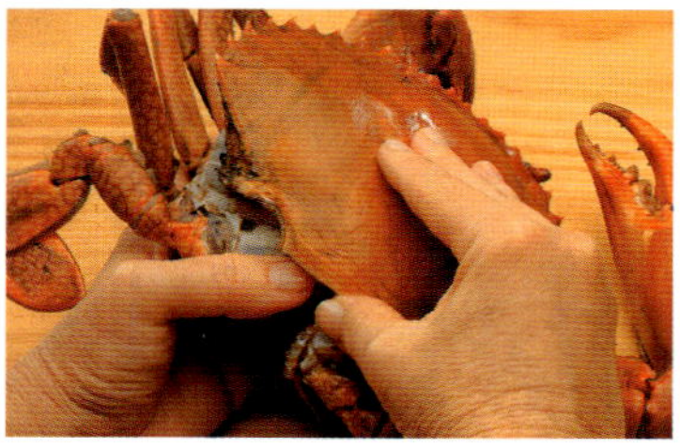

Pic 21

Pic 22

CLEANING CRABS

The most common crabs sold in Australia and New Zealand are the blue swimmer crab, mud crab, spanner crab and Moreton Bay bug. Southern king crab or Alaskan king crab are also available, but not in huge quantities.

Hard-Shelled Crabs (Mud Crab)

Wash and scrub under cold, running water. When clean, the entire crab may be poached or steamed. However, as most mud crabs are sold live, if you wish to cook the crab, you must first kill and disjoint it, then remove the edible parts.

To kill crab instantly, stab just behind the eyes with the point of a sharp knife. Another killing technique is to place crab in freezer for a few hours. (Pic 19)

Place crab on its back, and gently fold back tail flap or apron. Twist and pull off apron. You will find that the intestinal vein is attached and will pull out along with the apron. Discard. (Pic 20)

Hold the crab with one hand where the apron was removed. Use the other hand to pry-up the top shell. Tear-off and discard the top shell. (Pic 21)

Remove the gills, take out the greyish bag and pull out mandibles from front of crab.

Hold the body where the legs were attached, and apply pressure so that crab splits in half along the centre of its body. Fold back halves and twist apart. (Pic 22)

Twist off claws and legs where they join the body. Crack with hammer or nutcracker to make the meat easy to remove.

Soft-Shelled Crabs

Cut across the eyes with a sharp knife. Pull out and discard the stomach sac. Turn over and lift the flap or apron and fold it away from the body. Pull out the apron and attached intestinal vein, and discard. Turn crab right-side-up and lift flaps on each side near legs. Scrape off and discard spongy gills.

Pic 23

Pic 24

Pic 25

Pic 26

OPENING ABALONE

Using a strong knife, force the blade tip into the thin part of the shell underneath the flesh. Fork blade backwards and forwards until muscle is freed from shell. Lift out flesh, remove intestine and wash flesh well under cold, running water.

Slice off dark heel (sucker pad). Slice the flesh horizontally in two, wrap slices in tea towel and pound well with the side of a meat mallet or cleaver until limp and velvety. Slices can be cut into thin strips or chopped, depending on cooking method.

CLEANING PRAWNS

Most people prefer to remove the head and body shell before eating. However, the entire body of the prawn is edible, depending on the cooking method.

To peel, break off head, place finger on underside between legs, and roll prawn. The body shell will come away. Then squeeze tail section, and remainder of shell will slip off. (Pic 23)

Slit down the middle of the outside curve to expose the intestinal vein. Remove it, and wash prawn under cold, running water. It is not necessary to remove the vein from bay or smaller prawns. However, veins of larger prawns sometimes contain shell or grit that can interfere with taste. (Pic 24)

CLEANING YABBIES

Freshwater crayfish or yabbies can be found in many inland streams. They have very sweet meat in the tail. Usually they are cooked in their shells.

To remove the intestinal vein, hold on a firm surface, right-side-up. (Pic 25)

Hold firmly with one hand and pull the tail flap away from the yabby to remove the intestinal vein. (Pic 26)

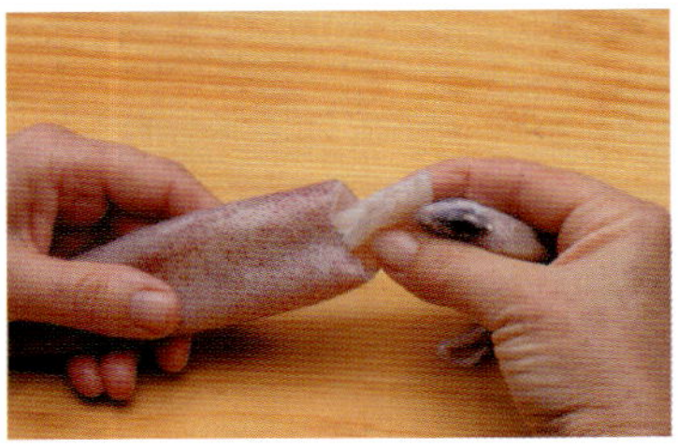

Pic 27

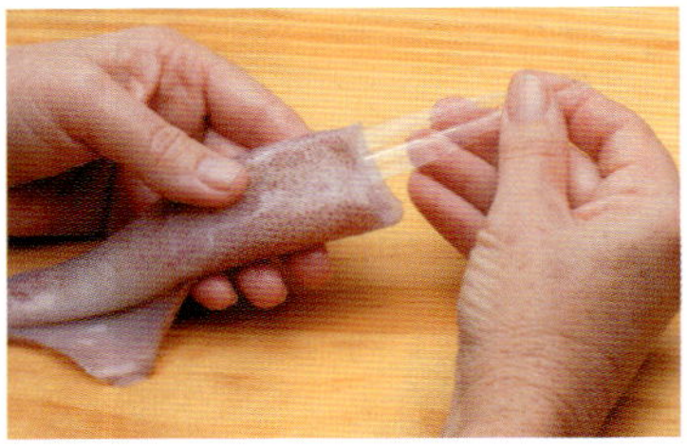

Pic 28

Pic 29

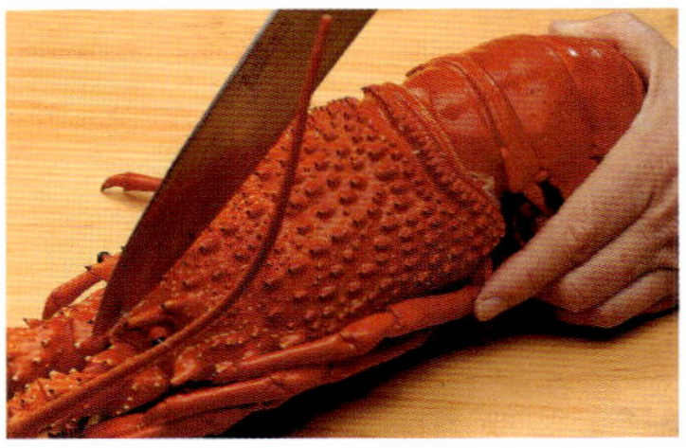

Pic 30

Pic 31

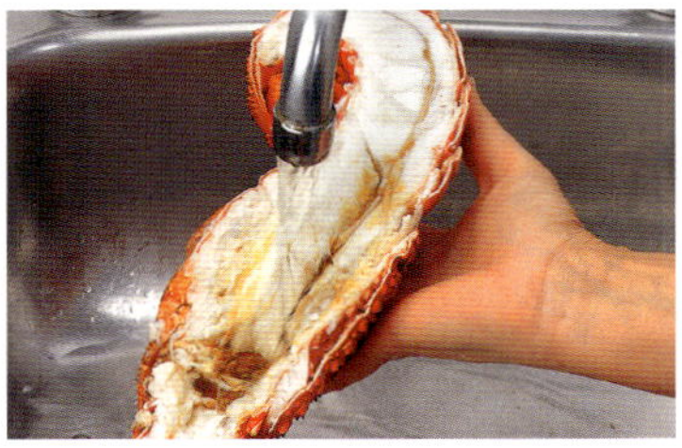

Pic 32

CLEANING SQUID

Squid can be poached, sautéd, fried, stuffed, baked and grilled. Do not overcook as it will become tough.

Rinse in cold water, and then cut off tentacles, just above the eye. Squeeze the thick centre part of the tentacles. This will push out the hard beak, which you should discard. (Pic 27)

Squeeze the entrails out by running your fingers from the closed to the open end. Pull out the quill and discard. (Pic 28)

Peel off skin by slipping finger under it. Pull off the edible fins from either side and also skin them. (Pic 29)

CLEANING LOBSTER

You can purchase whole lobster, either live, frozen and whole. Also available are uncooked frozen lobster tails and canned or frozen lobster meat.

To kill a live lobster, hold it on its back on a firm surface. With a heavy chef's knife, stab the point into the mouth to severe the spinal cord. You may also stun the lobster by placing it in the freezer for a period (about 30 minutes for each 500g).

Weigh to calculate cooking time. Place live lobster in a large pot of cold, salty water and bring to simmering point. Simmer, but do not boil, for 8 minutes per 500g weight.

Hold lobster right-side-up on a firm surface. Pierce the shell at the centre of the body behind the head. (Pic 30)

Cut lobster in half lengthwise, and remove and discard sac near the head and intestinal vein in the tail. Remove any mustard from the body and reserve for flavouring your sauces. (Pic 31)

Clean the lobster by rinsing under cold, running water. (Pic 32)

CLEANING OCTOPUS

Cut head from body section, just below the eyes, to remove tentacles. Cut out eyes and clean body cavity. Push beak up through centre of joined tentacles, cut off and dispose.

Wash thoroughly. Pay particular attention to tentacles as the suckers may contain sand.

Skin is difficult to remove from fresh octopus. Skin may be left on for cooking. However, to remove skin, parboil in a little water for 5 –10 minutes, then skin when cool enough to handle.

To clean small, whole octopus, cut up back of head and remove gut. Push beak up and cut out. Cut out eyes and wash thoroughly.

soups

San Franciscan Seafood Chowder in Bread Cups

Ingredients

8 smallish round loaves of bread

85g/3oz butter

2 leeks, well washed and finely sliced

2 onions, finely chopped

4 cloves garlic, minced

2 carrots, peeled and chopped

1 parsnip, peeled and chopped

2 stalks celery, finely sliced

1 tablespoon fresh thyme leaves

$^1/_2$ cup/60g/2oz plain flour

8 cups fish stock

1kg/2$^1/_4$ lb mixed seafood including prawns, mussels, clams, squid, white fish

200mL/7fl oz thick cream

$^1/_2$ bunch parsley, chopped

salt and pepper to taste

juice of 1 large lemon

$^1/_2$ bunch chives, chopped

Method

1. Preheat the oven to 200°C/400°F. First, prepare the bread cups. Using a sharp knife, cut a large hole in top of each bread loaf, then remove crusty top and set aside. Carefully remove all soft bread from inside of loaves, leaving the surrounding crust intact.

2. Place loaves in the preheated oven and bake for 15 minutes until the loaves are crisp and dry. Set aside.

3. Melt butter in a large saucepan, and add chopped leeks, onions, garlic, carrots, parsnip, celery and thyme leaves. Sauté in butter for 10 minutes until vegetables are soft and golden. Remove the pan from the heat, and sprinkle flour over vegetables, stirring constantly to mix the flour with butter. Return the pan to the heat and continue stirring until the mixture begins to turn golden (about 2 minutes). This gives flour a 'cooked' flavour.

4. Add fish stock, stirring constantly to dissolve the roux mixture into liquid, then simmer the chowder for 20 minutes. Meanwhile, prepare seafood by cutting the fish and shellfish into bite-sized pieces.

5. Add all seafood, cream, parsley and salt and pepper (to taste) to chowder, and cook for a further 5 minutes. Do not allow the chowder to boil rapidly because it may curdle. Once the shellfish has cooked, stir lemon juice through the chowder. Then, ladle the chowder into the bread cups. Garnish with chopped chives and serve.

Serves 8

American Shrimp Bisque

Ingredients

85g/3oz butter

3 tablespoons finely chopped onion

1 stalk celery, finely chopped

1 tablespoon plain flour

1kg/2¼ lb cooked prawns, shelled, deveined and chopped

3½ cups warm milk

½ cup double cream

2 tablespoons sherry

salt

freshly ground black pepper

paprika

freshly grated nutmeg

3 tablespoons chopped fresh parsley or snipped chives

Method

1. Melt butter in a saucepan over low heat, add onion and celery, and cover and cook for 5 minutes, taking care not to let vegetables brown.

2. Stir in flour and cook for 1 minute. Add prawns. Gradually stir in milk until blended. Bring to the boil, lower heat and cook, stirring, for 2 minutes or until soup thickens. Stir in double cream and heat through without boiling.

3. Stir sherry into soup and season to taste with salt, black pepper, paprika and nutmeg. Garnish servings with parsley or chives

Serves 4

Hot and Sour Prawn Soup

(opposite)

Ingredients

1kg/2¼ lb medium uncooked prawns

1 tablespoon vegetable oil

8 slices fresh or bottled galangal or fresh ginger

8 kaffir lime leaves

2 stalks fresh lemon grass, bruised, or

1 teaspoon dried lemon grass, soaked in hot water until soft

2 fresh red chillies, halved and seeded

8 cups water

3 tablespoons fresh coriander (cilantro) leaves

1 fresh red chilli, chopped

2 tablespoons lime juice

2 kaffir lime leaves, shredded

Method

1. Shell and devein prawns, and set aside. Reserve heads and shells. Heat oil in a large saucepan over a high heat, add prawn heads and shells and cook, stirring, for 5 minutes or until shells change colour. Stir in galangal or fresh ginger, lime leaves, lemon grass, halved chillies and water, cover and bring to simmering point. Simmer, stirring occasionally, for 15 minutes.

2. Strain liquid into a clean saucepan and discard solids. Add prawns and cook for 2 minutes. Stir in coriander (cilantro), chopped chilli and lime juice, and cook for 1 minute or until prawns are tender.

3. Ladle soup into bowls and garnish with shredded lime leaves.

Serves 4

Prawn and Chicken Soup

Ingredients

1 tablespoon vegetable oil

1 onion, diced

1 red capsicum (pepper), diced

2 cloves garlic, crushed

1 teaspoon finely chopped fresh ginger

4 cups chicken stock

125g/4½oz boneless chicken thigh or breast fillets, sliced

20 uncooked small prawns, shelled and deveined

125g/4½oz rice noodles

125g/4½oz canned bamboo shoots, drained and sliced

5 button mushrooms, thinly sliced

¼ lettuce, shredded

2 spring onions, thinly sliced

2 tablespoons finely chopped fresh coriander (cilantro)

1½ tablespoons soy sauce

freshly ground black pepper

Method

1. Heat oil in a saucepan over a medium heat, add onion and red capsicum (pepper) and cook, stirring, for 5 minutes or until onion is soft. Add garlic and ginger and cook for 2 minutes longer.

2. Stir in stock and bring to the boil. Add chicken, prawns, noodles, bamboo shoots and mushrooms, reduce heat and simmer for 5 minutes or until noodles are tender.

3. Stir in lettuce, spring onions, coriander (cilantro), soy sauce and black pepper to taste and serve immediately.

Serves 4

Mussel Soup

Ingredients

1kg/$2\frac{1}{4}$lb mussels, cleaned and scrubbed

1 small onion, sliced

1 stalk celery, sliced

1 clove garlic, chopped

$\frac{1}{2}$ cup white wine

285mL/10fl oz water

1 small carrot, diced finely

55g/2oz cauliflower, divided into florets

$\frac{1}{2}$ red capsicum (pepper), diced finely

$\frac{1}{2}$ onion, diced finely

1 pinch saffron

10 coriander seeds, cracked

45mL/$1\frac{1}{2}$fl oz sherry vinegar

55g/2oz butter

2 tablespoons plain flour

2 tablespoons double cream

salt and pepepr to taste

fresh parsley and snipped chives

Method

1. Put mussels in a casserole with small onions, celery, garlic and white wine.

2. Cook until mussels have opened; stir frequently to make sure mussels are cooked evenly. Remove mussels and set aside. Strain broth and set aside.

3. In a large saucepan on high heat put water, carrot, cauliflower, red capsicum (pepper), onion, saffron and coriander. Bring to the boil and add sherry vinegar. Remove from heat and allow to cool. When cold strain vegetables from the cooking liquid. Reserve vegetables and cooking liquid.

4. In a saucepan on medium heat, melt butter, then add flour; stir with a wooden spoon and cook gently for 2 minutes. Add broth and cooking liquid, whisking with a whisk, and cook until slightly thickened and a smooth consistency.

3. Add reserved vegetables, mussels and cream and bring to the boil. Taste for seasoning and rectify if necessary with salt and pepper. Add parsley and chives just before serving.

Serves 4

Prawn Bisque

Ingredients

315g/11oz cooked prawns, shelled and deveined

1/2 onion, diced

1/2 cup tomato paste

2 1/2 cups chicken stock

1/2 cup double cream

1/4 teaspoon paprika

freshly ground black pepper

1-2 tablespoons dry sherry

snipped chives, for garnish

Method

1. Place prawns, onion and tomato paste in a food processor or blender and process to make a purée. With machine running, slowly add stock and process to combine.

2. Place prawn mixture in a saucepan and cook over a low heat, stirring frequently, for 10 minutes or until the mixture comes to the boil.

3. Stir in double cream, paprika and black pepper to taste and cook for 2 minutes or until heated through. Stir in sherry, garnish with snipped chives and serve immediately.

Serves 6

Spanish Fish Soup with Saffron

Ingredients

2 tablespoons olive oil

2 large carrots, finely chopped

3 leeks, finely sliced and well washed

1 red capsicum (pepper), chopped

1 green capsicum (pepper), chopped

1 tablespoon Spanish paprika

large pinch saffron threads

2 cups white wine

3 cups fish stock

400g/14oz firm white fish fillets, diced

400g/14oz prawns, shelled and deveined

400g/14oz baby calamari or squid

2 tablespoons chopped parsley

1 lemon, cut into 6 wedges

Method

1. Heat olive oil in a large saucepan and add carrots, leeks and capsicums (peppers) and sauté until softened (about 10 minutes). Add paprika and saffron, continuing to cook for a few more minutes.

2. Add wine and stock, and bring the soup to the boil, simmering for 15 minutes. Add diced fish, shelled prawns and squid and simmer for a further 5 minutes. Sprinkle with parsley, and serve with a wedge of lemon.

Serves 6

Spicy Prawn Soup

Ingredients

4 cups fish stock

5cm/2in piece fresh galangal, sliced or 8 pieces dried galangal

8 kaffir lime leaves

2 stalks fresh lemon grass, finely chopped or 1 teaspoon dried lemon grass, soaked in hot water until soft

2 tablespoons lime juice

2 tablespoons finely sliced lime rind

2 tablespoons Thai fish sauce (*nam pla*)

2 tablespoons Thai red curry paste

500g/1 lb uncooked large prawns, shelled and deveined, tails left intact

3 spring onions, sliced diagonally

3 tablespoons fresh coriander (cilantro) leaves

1 small fresh red chilli, sliced

Method

1. Place stock in a large saucepan and bring to the boil over a medium heat. Add galangal, lime leaves, lemon grass, lime juice, lime rind, fish sauce and red curry paste and simmer, stirring occasionally, for 10 minutes.

2. Add prawns and spring onions, and simmer for 5 minutes longer or until prawns are cooked.

3. Remove galangal and discard. Sprinkle soup with coriander (cilantro) leaves and sliced chilli and serve.

Serves 4

French Mussel Soup

Ingredients

500g/1 lb mussels

1 small onion, chopped

1 shallot, chopped

1 clove garlic, crushed

1/2 cup finely chopped parsley

freshly ground black pepper

75g/2 1/2 oz butter or margarine

1 1/2 cups white wine

1 1/2 tablespoons lemon juice

Method

1. Scrubmussels thoroughly and place in a saucepan with onion, shallot, garlic, parsley, black pepper, half the butter or margarine and the wine. Cover and cook mussels for a few minutes over a high heat. Shake in the pan several times to ensure even cooking.

2. When mussels have opened, transfer to a heated serving dish and keep warm. Strain the liquid into a small saucepan and reduce over a high heat until only half remains.

3. Remove from the heat, and whisk in the remaining butter or margarine. When thick and foamy, whisk in lemon juice and pour over mussels. Serve very hot with chunks of fresh, crusty French bread.

Serves 4

Fish Noodle Soup

Ingredients

500g/1 lb white fish fillets

vegetable oil

85g/3oz spring onions

1 teaspoon chopped, fresh ginger

1 teaspoon garlic, chopped or crushed

1 red capsicum, seeded and chopped

4 cups fish stock or water

1 tablespoon oyster sauce

1/2 teaspoon ground black pepper

1 teaspoon sesame oil

1 tablespoon dry sherry

225g/8oz egg noodles, boiled

1 teaspoon sesame oil, extra

1/2 red capsicum, seeded (extra) and chopped for garnish

Method

1. Chop fish into bite-sized pieces. Heat enough vegetable oil to deep-fry fish for 2 1/2 minutes. Remove and drain. Cut spring onions into 4cm/1 1/2 in sections, separating white parts from green.

2. Heat 3 tablespoons of oil and brown ginger and soften garlic. Add fish, capsicum and white sections of spring onions. Stir-fry for 3 minutes then add stock or water and boil. Add green spring onion sections, oyster sauce, black pepper, oil and sherry and simmer for 1 minute, stirring.

3. Add hot, cooked, drained noodles and extra 1 teaspoon of oil. Stir through until hot. Serve immediately, garnished with chopped capsicum.

Serves 4

Chunky Corn and Prawn Gazpacho

Ingredients

4 large roma tomatoes, washed and halved

1 yellow capsicum (pepper), seeded and quartered

$^1/_4$–$^1/_2$ teaspoon Tabasco sauce

1 teaspoon salt, or to taste

2 ears corn

1 small leek, white parts only

1 clove garlic, peeled

1 small red onion

1 tablespoon olive oil

2 teaspoons mild sweet paprika

500g/1 lb shelled raw king prawns, tails on

juice of two limes

2 tablespoons chopped fresh parsley

$^1/_3$ cup fresh coriander (cilantro) leaves

lime wedges

Method

1. First, make the spicy sauce. Process tomatoes in a food processor briefly, then pour the mixture into a large bowl. Process yellow capsicum (pepper) pieces until finely chopped and add these to the tomatoes. Add Tabasco sauce and salt to taste. Set aside in the refrigerator for an hour or up to eight hours.

2. Using a sharp knife, cut corn off the ears. Heat a heavy frypan over a high heat, then add corn and 'dry fry' until it is slightly charred and golden brown. Pour into a small bowl and set aside.

3. Wash leek thoroughly, then place the white parts only, garlic and onion in a food processor and chop finely. Alternatively, chop finely with a knife. To the frypan, add oil and heat. Then add finely chopped leek, onion and garlic mixture and the paprika and sauté over a medium heat for 5 minutes or until the vegetables have softened and begun to turn gold around the edges.

4. Move onion mixture to the side of the pan and add raw prawns. Allow prawns to cook for a moment or two until they are orange in colour underneath, then turn them over and cook the other side.

5. Bring onion mixture in from the side of the pan and toss with prawns. Add prawn mixture to chilled tomato mixture and toss thoroughly. Add half charred corn and lime juice and parsley and mix well before returning to the fridge to chill.

6. To serve, divide the gazpacho among 6 martini glasses or wine goblets and top with coriander (cilantro) leaves, remaining charred corn and lime wedges.

Serves 6

Prawn and Crab Soup

(opposite)

Ingredients

6 tomatoes, chopped

2 onions, chopped

1 tablespoon vegetable oil

4 cloves garlic, crushed

1 tablespoon oregano leaves

2 fresh coriander (cilantro) bunches

1 fish head, such snapper, perch, cod or haddock

10 cups water

2 uncooked crabs, cleaned and cut into serving pieces

12 medium uncooked prawns, shelled and deveined

170g/6oz fish fillet, cut into chunks

Method

1. Place tomatoes and onions in a food processor or blender and process to make a purée.

2. Heat oil in a saucepan over medium heat, add garlic and cook, stirring, for 1 minute or until golden. Stir in tomato mixture, then add oregano leaves and coriander (cilantro) bunches, bring to simmering and simmer for 15 minutes. Add fish head and water and simmer for 20 minutes. Strain stock and discard solids. Return stock to a clean saucepan.

3. Add crabs and prawns to stock, bring to simmering point and simmer for 3 minutes. Add fish and simmer for 1–2 minutes or until all seafood is cooked.

Serves 6

Prawn and Crab Soup

Tom Yam Gong

Ingredients

3 cups fish stock

1 tablespoon chopped fresh lemon grass or 1 teaspoon dried lemon grass

$^1/_2$ teaspoon finely grated lemon rind

2 tablespoons Thai fish sauce *(nam pla)*

255g/9oz button mushrooms, sliced

500g/1 lb large uncooked prawns, shelled and deveined

$^1/_3$ cup double cream

115g/4oz bean sprouts

2 spring onions, cut into 2cm/$^3/_4$ in lengths

1 teaspoon chilli paste (*sambal oelek*)

$^1/_3$ cup lemon juice

3 tablespoons chopped fresh coriander (cilantro)

freshly ground black pepper

Method

1. Place stock in a large saucepan and bring to the boil. Stir in lemon grass, lemon rind, fish sauce, mushrooms and prawns, and cook for 3–4 minutes or until prawns change colour.

2. Reduce heat to low and stir in double cream and cook for 2–3 minutes or until heated through.

3. Remove the pan from heat, and add bean sprouts, spring onions, chilli paste (*sambal oelek*), lemon juice, coriander and black pepper to taste. Serve immediately.

Serves 4

Clam Chowder

Clam Chowder

(opposite)

Ingredients

255g/9oz butter

6 slices of bacon, finely chopped

3 onions, finely chopped

1 stalk celery, finely chopped

1 cup plain flour

5 cups milk

3 cups fish stock

5 potatoes, boiled and finely diced

1 kg/2¼ lb clam meat

salt and pepper

snipped chives

cream

whole clams, steamed open for garnish

Method

1. Melt butter in a saucepan, and add bacon, onion and celery. Cook for 5 minutes or until tender. Add flour and cook, stirring, for 2 minutes.

2. Add milk, fish stock and potatoes, and cover and simmer for 10 minutes. Add clam meat and cook more for 10 minutes. Season to taste.

5. Serve, scattered with sipped chives, in a deep plate with cream, parsley and clams in shell.

Serves 8 – 10

Mussel Bisque

Ingredients

500g/1 lb flounder, or any white fish fillets

3 cups milk

salt and pepper

⅛ teaspoon nutmeg

1 bay leaf

1 jar mussels

2 tablespoons butter

1 medium-sized onion, finely chopped

2 stalks celery, finely chopped

3 tablespoons flour

1 tablespoon lemon juice

1 tablespoon finely chopped parsley or chives

¼ cup cream

croutons to serve

Method

1. Cut fish fillets into 2cm/¾in squares. Place in a saucepan with milk, salt, pepper, nutmeg and bay leaf. Bring gently to the boil, then simmer slowly for 10 minutes. Stand covered for 10 minutes to infuse flavour. Strain milk from fish and reserve; keep fish warm.

2. Drain liquid from mussels and rinse in cold water, then cut into 2 or 3 pieces.

3. Melt butter in a large saucepan, add onion and celery and cook gently without browning. When soft, stir in the flour and cook for 1 minute while stirring.

4. Remove the saucepan from heat and gradually add reserved milk, stirring well after each addition until mixture is free from lumps. Return to heat and stir until mixture boils and thickens.

5. Add lemon juice, chopped mussels, chopped parsley and cooked fish. Simmer slowly for 10 minutes. Stir in cream and simmer 5 more minutes. Serve in individual bowls with croutons.

Serves 4 – 6

Maltese Mussels

Ingredients

85mL/3fl oz olive oil

1 medium onion, chopped finely

3 garlic cloves, chopped

2 roasted capsicums (peppers), peeled and diced

2 tomatoes, diced

1/2 bulb fennel, diced

1/2 celery stalk , diced

145mL/5fl oz white wine

1 orange, juiced and zest grated

200mL/7fl oz tomato juice

2 cups chicken stock

salt, pepper, cayenne pepper and paprika

500g/1 lb black mussels, cleaned

1 spring onion, sliced

Method

1. In a large saucepan on medium heat, add oil, onion, garlic, capsicum, tomato, fennel, celery and cook for 10 minutes.

2. Add white wine, orange juice, zest, tomato juice, chicken stock and seasoning, and cook for 20 minutes.

3. Add mussels and cook until all mussels have opened, about 8–10 minutes

4. Top with spring onion, and serve with wood fired bread or Grissini.

Serves 4

Creamy Oyster Bisque

Ingredients

20 fresh oysters, shucked or 1 jar (about 20 oysters), drained, liquid reserved

1 cup fish or vegetable stock

1/2 cup white wine

1 small white onion or 1/2 leek, diced

1 stalk celery, diced

2 cups diced peeled potato

1 tablespoon chopped fresh thyme or 1 teaspoon dried thyme

1/2 cup milk

freshly ground black pepper

sprigs watercress or fresh parsley, optional

Method

1. Add liquid from oysters to the stock.

2. Heat 2 tablespoons of the wine in a large saucepan over a low heat. Add onion or leek and celery, and cook, stirring, for 4–5 minutes or until onion is transparent. Add potato and thyme, stir in stock mixture and remaining wine, and bring to simmering pint. Simmer for 10–15 minutes or until potatoes are soft and most of the liquid is absorbed. Cool slightly.

3. Transfer mixture to a food processor or blender. Add half the oysters, milk and black pepper to taste and purée. Return mixture to a clean saucepan and bring to the boil. Remove soup from heat, and stir in remaining oysters.

4. To serve, ladle soup into warm bowls and top with watercress or parsley sp-igs, if desired.

Serves 4

Mussel, Witlof and Basil Soup

Ingredients

1 kg/2$^{1}/_{4}$ lb black mussels

1 small onion, sliced

1 stalk celery, sliced

1 garlic clove, chopped

200mL/7fl oz white wine

2 witlof or Belgian endives, with leaves cut loose

30g/1oz butter

2 tablespoon double cream or thickened cream

15 basil leaves, chopped finely

salt and pepper

Method

1. Put mussels in a saucepan with onion, celery, garlic and white wine. Cook until mussels have opened; stir frequently to make sure mussels are cooked evenly. Remove mussels and set aside. Strain broth and set aside.

2. Melt butter in a saucepan and stir-fry witlofs. Add broth, cream and basil, and whisk until ingredients are blended.

5. Add mussels, and heat until boiling. season to taste and serve in individual bowls.

Serves 4

Lobster Bisque

Ingredients

1 small lobster, cooked

1 large carrot, peeled and diced

1 small onion, finely chopped

115g/4oz butter

$^{3}/_{4}$ cup dry white wine

bouquet garni

6 cups fish or chicken stock

$^{1}/_{2}$ cup rice

salt, pepper and ground cayenne pepper

$^{1}/_{2}$ cup cream

2 tablespoons brandy

chopped parsley

Method

1. Split lobster in half lengthwise, remove flesh from shell and set aside. Wrap shell in an old tea towel, crush with a hammer and set aside. Sauté carrot and onion in half the butter until softened without colouring, or for 5 minutes. Add crushed shell, sauté a further minute or so, then add wine. Boil hard until reduced by half.

2. Add bouquet garni, stock and rice. After about 20 minutes, when the rice is tender, remove the large pieces of shell and bouquet garni. Purée in a food processor with remainder of butter, doing so in small batches. Pour through a strainer. Rinse out the food processor to remove every trace of shell and purée the strained liquid again, this time with lobster flesh, saving a few pieces for the garnish.

3. Reheat gently. Taste, add salt, pepper and cayenne to taste, then stir in cream, brandy and reserved lobster pieces cut into thin slices. Serve very hot, garnished with parsley.

Serves 8 – 10

Crab and Sweet Corn Soup

Ingredients

6 cups strong chicken stock

170g/6oz can crab meat

425g/15oz canned cream style sweet corn

$^1/_2$ teaspoon salt

$^1/_2$ teaspoon sesame oil

1 tablespoon dry sherry

4 shallots, finely chopped

1 tablespoon cornflour

1 tablespoon water

Method

1. Bring stock to the boil in a large saucepan then turn heat down to a simmer.

2. Drain and flake crab meat and add to stock with creamed corn, salt and sesame oil. Simmer for 10 minutes.

3. Add sherry and shallots. Blend cornflour with water and stir into soup.

4. Stir until soup thickens, and serve immediately.

Serves 6

Rustic Mediterranean Seafood Soup

Rustic Mediterranean Seafood Soup

(opposite)

Ingredients

200g/7oz calamari tubes, cleaned

300g/10½oz green prawns

200g/7oz mussels

255g/9oz mixed firm white fish fillets (red mullet, sea perch, red fish)

1 tablespoon olive oil

2 cloves garlic, crushed

1 onion, finely chopped

½ cup white wine

400g/14oz canned diced tomatoes

4 cups fish stock

pinch saffron

2 potatoes, peeled and cut into large cubes

Method

1. Cut calamari tubes into rings. Peel and devein prawns, leaving the tails intact. Scrub mussels and debeard, discarding any that are already open. Remove any bones from fish and cut into large pieces.

2. Heat oil in a large saucepan. Add garlic and onion and cook over a medium heat for 3 minutes or until onion is golden. Add white wine and bring to the boil. Cook over a high heat until nearly all the liquid has been absorbed.

3. Add tomatoes, fish stock, saffron and potatoes and simmer for 15 minutes or until potatoes are tender. Do not overcook or potatoes will start to break up.

4. Add all seafood and simmer for 3–5 minutes or until tender. Serve with crusty Italian bread.

Serves 6

Thai Prawn Soup with Lemon Grass

Ingredients

300g/10½oz large green prawns

3 stalks lemon grass

1 litre fish stock

2cm/¾ in piece ginger, peeled and cut into fine strips

2 kaffir lime leaves

½ small pineapple, peeled and cored

1 tablespoon fish sauce

1 tablespoon lime juice

6 spring onions, thinly sliced on the diagonally

fresh coriander (cilantro) leaves

pepper to taste

Method

1. Peel and devein prawns, leaving tails intact. Reserve shells and discard veins. Halve lemon grass stalks and squash the bases with the flat side of a knife.

2. Place prawn shells in a medium saucepan with stock and bring slowly to the boil. Reduce the heat and simmer gently for 10 minutes. Strain, return to the saucepan and add lemon grass, ginger and lime leaves and return to simmering point.

3. Cut pineapple into thin pieces and add to stock along with prawns. Simmer just until prawns turn pink and tender (a few minutes, depending on their size). Add fish sauce, lime juice, spring onions and coriander.

4. Remove lemon grass and lime leaves, season with pepper and serve immediately with a wedge of lime.

Serves 6

Crab Soup

Ingredients

170g/6oz canned crabmeat (or fresh, picked crabmeat)

1 egg

4 dried Chinese mushrooms

85g/3oz canned bamboo shoots

1 leek

small piece fresh ginger

1 tablespoon vegetable oil

2 teaspoons soy sauce

1 tablespoon mirin or dry sherry

6 cups chicken or fish stock , or water

2 teaspoons salt

freshly ground pepper

$1^{1}/_{2}$ tablespoons cornflour

2 tablespoons chopped parsley

Method

1. Drain crabmeat and break up. Beat egg in a small bowl.

2. Soak dried mushrooms in water for 20 minutes and discard stalks and slice caps. Drain bamboo shoots and cut into strips. Slit leek almost through, discarding tough green part and wash carefully, then cut into strips. Grate or finely chop ginger.

3. Heat oil in a wok or saucepan and add the mushrooms, leek, bamboo shoots and ginger and stir-fry for a minute.

4. Add crabmeat, sprinkle with soy sauce and rice wine and pour in the heated stock or water. As soon as the liquid comes to the boil, skim off any scum. Season with salt and pepper and stir in the cornflour mixed with a little water to thicken the soup.

5. Pour in beaten egg and mix, stirring lightly so that the egg sets in short strands. Sprinkle with chopped parsley and serve.

Serves 4 – 6

Pipi and Black Mussel Broth

Ingredients

45mL/1$^{1}/_{2}$fl oz vegetable oil

1 onion, finely chopped

2 tablespoons Tom Yum paste

200g/7oz pipis, cleaned and sandless

200g/7oz mussels, cleaned

4 cups chicken stock

1 stalk lemon grass, chopped

1 lime, juiced

1 tablespoon coriander (cilantro) stalk and roots, finely chopped

1 tablespoon Thai fish sauce (*nam pla)*

1 tablespoon fresh coriander (cilantro) leaves, roughly chopped

Method

1. In a wok or a large saucepan, on high heat, add oil, onion, Tom Yum paste, pipis and mussels and simmer with a lid for 30 seconds.

2. Add chicken stock, lemon grass, lime juice, coriander stalk and roots, Thai fish sauce and stir through. Cook until all shells have opened.

3. Add fresh coriander leaves and serve in soup bowls.

Serves 4

Manhattan Chowder

Ingredients

2kg/4½ lb mussels, cleaned

1 cup water

145mL/5fl oz white wine

4 rashers bacon, rind removed and diced

1 large onion, chopped

1 bay leaf

1 green capsicum (pepper), finely diced

2 stalks celery, diced

500g/1 lb peeled and diced potatoes

2 x 400g/14oz cans peeled tomatoes, seeds removed, chopped
Tabasco sauce

Method

1. Wash and scrub mussels and steam them open. Remove and discard the shells, reserving mussels. Strain the cooking liquor through fine muslin and add enough water to measure 4 cups.

2. In a heavy saucepan cook bacon gently until it begins to crisp. Add onion and bay leaf and sauté until onion is tender. Add the capsicum (pepper) and celery, and sauté for a few more minutes.

3. Add potatoes and tomatoes with the juice, the mussel cooking liquid, and salt and pepper to taste. Bring to the boil and simmer, covered for 20 minutes, until potatoes are tender. Discard bay leaf, add mussels and cook a further 5-10 minutes. Season the chowder with a little Tabasco and serve.

Serves 6

Mussel Soup in a White Wine and Roasted Tomato Sauce

Ingredients

$1\frac{1}{2}$ kg/$3\frac{1}{3}$ lb mussels

340g/12oz tomatoes

75mL/$2\frac{1}{2}$ fl oz olive oil

4 cloves garlic, crushed

1 brown onion, chopped

$\frac{1}{2}$ cup white wine

400g/14oz can tomatoes, peeled

55mL/2oz tomato paste

85mL/3fl oz fish stock, or water

2 tablespoons oregano, chopped

salt and pepper

Method

1. Wash mussels under water, scrub shells with a scourer, and remove beards. Discard any mussels that are open.

2. Place halved tomatoes on a baking tray, drizzle with a little olive oil, sprinkle with salt, and roast in the oven for 20 minutes.

3. Heat oil in a saucepan and sauté garlic and onion until soft. Add the white wine and cook for 2 minutes. Add roasted tomatoes, can of tomatoes, tomato paste, stock (or water) and chopped oregano and simmer for 5–10 minutes. Season with salt and pepper. Add mussels, cover, and cook for a further 5 minutes, until mussels have opened. Discard any that do not open.

4. Serve soup with crusty Italian bread.

Serves 4 – 6

Prawn and Wonton Soup

Ingredients

10 cups chicken stock

1 carrot, cut into thin strips

1 stalk celery, cut into thin strips

$\frac{1}{2}$ red capsicum (pepper), cut into thin strips

24 large cooked prawns, shelled and deveined

PORK WONTONS:

255g/9oz pork mince

1 egg, lightly beaten

2 spring onions, chopped

1 fresh red chilli, seeded and chopped

1 tablespoon soy sauce

1 tablespoon oyster sauce

24 spring roll or wonton wrappers, each $12\frac{1}{2}$ cm/5in square

Method

1. To make wontons, place pork, egg, spring onions, chilli, soy sauce and oyster sauce in a bowl and mix to combine.

2. Place spoonfuls of mixture in the centre of each spring roll or wonton wrapper, then draw the corners together and twist to form small bundles. Place wontons in a steamer set over a saucepan of boiling water and steam for 3–4 minutes or until wontons are cooked.

3. Place chicken stock in a saucepan and bring to the boil over a medium heat. Add carrot, celery and red capsicum (pepper) and simmer for 1 minute. Add prawns and cook for 1 minute longer.

4. To serve, place 3–4 wontons in each soup bowl and carefully ladle over soup. Serve immediately.

Serves 6 – 8

salads

Sri Lankan Prawn Salad

Ingredients

1 kg/2¼ lb large cooked prawns, shelled and deveined

1 grapefruit, segmented

1 orange, segmented

2 bananas, peeled and sliced

1 onion, sliced

6 spinach leaves, shredded

30g/1oz cashews, chopped

DRESSING:

2 tablespoons lemon juice

1 cup natural yoghurt

1 teaspoon curry powder

2 tablespoons mayonnaise

Method

1. Place prawns, grapefruit, orange, bananas, onion and spinach in a salad bowl. Set aside.

2. To make dressing, place lemon juice, yoghurt, curry powder and mayonnaise in a bowl and mix to combine.

3. Spoon dressing over salad and toss. Sprinkle over cashews. Cover and chill.

Serves 6

Peach and Prawn Entrée Salad

(opposite)

Ingredients

200g/7oz dried peaches

1 tablespoon lemon juice

2 teaspoons lemon zest, grated

2 teaspoons brown sugar

1/2 teaspoon salt

1/2 teaspoon freshly ground black pepper

1/3 cup sherry vinegar

2 drops Tabasco sauce

500g/1 lb salad mix

2 teaspoons Dijon mustard

1 egg

2/3 cup light olive oil

12 king prawns, shelled and deveined

Method

1. Place dried peaches in a flat dish. Mix next 7 ingredients together and pour over peaches. Allow to stand at room temperature for 30 minutes.

2. Remove peaches from vinegar mixture. Pour the vinegar mixture into a blender or food processor, add mustard and egg, and process until smooth. With the motor running, add oil in a thin, steady stream. Dressing will become creamy and thicken slightly.

3. Divide salad mix between 4 plates and place 2 peach halves on slope of salad and arrange 3 prawns on each plate. Spoon dressing over salad and serve immediately.

Serves 4

Prawn and Avocado Salad

Ingredients

750g/1⅔ lb cooked king prawns

1 avocado, sliced

1 grapefruit, segmented

DRESSING:

2 tablespoons mayonnaise

2 tablespoons sour cream

1 tablespoon yoghurt

2 tablespoons chopped mint

Method

1. Shell and devein prawns. Arrange prawns, avocado and grapefruit on a serving plate.

2. To make dressing, combine mayonnaise, sour cream, yoghurt and mint. Drizzle over prawns, and serve immediately.

Serves 4

Mediterranean Salad

Ingredients

200g/7oz couscous

2 cups boiling water

1 tablespoon olive oil

1 tablespoon balsamic vinegar

freshly ground black pepper

1 cucumber, sliced

1 green capsicum (pepper), chopped

3 plum (egg or Italian) tomatoes, chopped

12 sun-dried tomatoes, sliced

55g/2oz marinated artichokes, drained and sliced

55g/2oz pitted black olives, sliced

200g/7oz cooked prawns, shelled and deveined (optional)

115g/4oz feta cheese, cut into 2cm/$^{3}/_{4}$ in cubes

2 tablespoons chopped fresh basil or 2 teaspoons dried basil

2 teaspoons finely grated lime or lemon rind

Method

1. Place couscous in a bowl, pour over boiling water and toss with a fork until couscous absorbs all the liquid. Add oil, vinegar and black pepper to taste and toss to combine. Set aside.

2. Place cucumber, green capsicum (pepper), fresh and sun-dried tomatoes, artichokes, olives, prawns (if using), feta cheese, basil and lime or lemon rind in a salad bowl and toss to combine. Add couscous mixture and toss.

Serves 4

Seafood Paella Salad

Ingredients

4 cups chicken stock

500g/1 lb uncooked large prawns

1 uncooked lobster tail (optional)

500g/1 lb mussels in shells, cleaned

2 tablespoons olive oil

1 onion, chopped

2 ham steaks, cut into 1cm/$^1/_2$in cubes

2 cups rice

$^1/_2$ teaspoon ground turmeric

115g/4oz fresh or frozen peas

1 red capsicum (pepper), diced

GARLIC DRESSING:

$^1/_2$ cup olive oil

$^1/_4$ cup white wine vinegar

3 tablespoons mayonnaise

2 cloves garlic, crushed

2 tablespoons chopped fresh parsley

freshly ground black pepper

Method

1. Place stock in a large saucepan and bring to the boil. Add prawns and cook for 1–2 minutes or until prawns change colour. Remove and set aside. Add lobster tail and cook for 5 minutes or until lobster changes colour and is cooked. Remove and set aside. Add mussels and cook until shells open - discard any mussels that do not open after 5 minutes. Remove and set aside. Strain stock and reserve. Peel and devein prawns, leaving tails intact. Refrigerate seafood until just prior to serving.

2. Heat oil in a large saucepan, and add onion and cook for 4–5 minutes or until soft. Add ham, rice and turmeric and cook, stirring, for 2 minutes. Add reserved stock and bring to the boil. Reduce heat, cover and simmer for 15 minutes or until liquid is absorbed and rice is cooked and dry. Stir in peas and red capsicum (pepper) and set aside to cool. Cover and refrigerate for at least 2 hours.

3. To make dressing, place oil, vinegar, mayonnaise, garlic, parsley and black pepper to taste in a food processor or blender and process to combine.

4. To serve, place seafood and rice in a large salad bowl, spoon over dressing and toss to combine.

Serves 4

Scandinavian Mussels

Ingredients

100mL/3½ fl oz water

½ onion, chopped finely

½ stalk celery, chopped finely

½ red capsicum (pepper), chopped finely

1 tablespoon sugar

2 tablespoons white vinegar

1 kg/2¼ lb black mussels, cleaned (*cooked mariniere style and removed from shell, see page 237*)

4 tablespoons mayonnaise

4 tablespoons chopped parsley

juice of 1 lemon

salt and pepper to taste

Method

1. In a small saucepan, bring water, onion, celery, red capsicum (pepper), sugar and vinegar to the boil for 1 minute. Remove vegetables from liquid and set aside to cool. Discard liquid.

2. Mix mussels, mayonnaise, vegetables, parsley and lemon juice in a bowl, and add salt and pepper to taste.

4. Serve cold with a green salad or a cold potato salad.

Serves 2

Tomato, Corn and Prawn Salad

Ingredients

2 cups cooked corn kernels

1 onion, finely sliced

200g/7oz cooked prawns, shelled, deveined and cut into 1cm/$^1/_2$ in lengths

2 tomatoes, chopped

55g/2oz spring onions, chopped

1 red capsicum (pepper), seeded and finely chopped

2 tablespoons red wine vinegar

2 tablespoons olive oil

1 clove garlic, crushed

1 tablespoon fresh lemon juice

chopped fresh parsley

Method

1. In a large bowl, combine corn, onion, prawns, tomatoes, spring onions and red capsicum (pepper), and mix well.

2. Mix together vinegar, oil, garlic and lemon juice and toss through salad. Serve topped with fresh parsley.

Serves 4

Chargrilled Baby Octopus Salad

Ingredients

340g/12oz baby octopus, cleaned

1 teaspoon sesame oil

1 tablespoon lime juice

$^{1}/_{4}$ cup sweet chilli sauce

1 tablespoon Thai fish sauce (*nam pla*)

55g/2oz rice vermicelli

115g/4oz mixed salad leaves

1 cup bean sprouts

1 Lebanese cucumber, halved

200g/7oz cherry tomatoes, halved

1 bunch coriander (cilantro) sprigs

lime wedges, to serve

Method

1. Rinse cleaned octopus and pat dry with paper towel.

2. Put sesame oil, lime juice, sweet chilli sauce and fish sauce in a jug and whisk to combine. Pour over octopus to coat. Cover with plastic wrap and marinate for 4 hours or overnight. Drain and reserve marinade.

3. Put vermicelli in a bowl, cover with boiling water and allow to stand for 10 minutes or until soft. Drain well.

4. Divide mixed salad leaves among four plates, and add bean sprouts, rice vermicelli, cucumber and cherry tomato.

5. Cook the octopus on a preheated chargrill or barbecue until tender and well coloured. Put the marinade in a small pot and bring to the boil. Serve the octopus on top of the salad, drizzle with the hot marinade and garnish with coriander and lime wedges.

Serves 4-6

Barbecued Seafood Salad (opposite)

Ingredients

2 tablespoons lemon juice

1 tablespoon olive oil

300g/10½ oz firm white fish (swordfish, mackerel or cod, cut into 2½cm/1in cubes

300g/10½ oz pink fish (salmon, ocean trout, marlin or tuna)

12 scallops

12 uncooked prawns (with or without shell)

1 calamari (squid), cleaned and tube cut into rings

1 large onion, cut into rings

1 telegraph cucumber, sliced thinly

1 bunch watercress, broken into sprigs

RASPBERRY AND TARRAGON DRESSING:

3 tablespoons chopped fresh tarragon

2 tablespoons raspberry or red wine vinegar

2 tablespoons lemon juice

1 tablespoon olive oil

freshly ground black pepper

Method

1. Place lemon juice and oil in a bowl. Whisk to combine. Add white and pink fish, scallops, prawns and calamari. Toss to combine. Cover. Marinate in the refrigerator for 1 hour or until ready to use. Do not marinate for longer than 2 hours.

2. Preheat a barbecue or char-grill pan until very hot. Drain seafood mixture and place on barbecue hotplate or in pan. Add onion. Cook, turning several times, for 6–8 minutes or until seafood is just cooked. Take care not to overcook or the seafood will be tough and dry. Transfer cooked seafood to a bowl and cool, then add cucumber.

3. Line a serving platter with watercress, and arrange seafood and cucumber on top.

4. To make dressing, place tarragon, vinegar, lemon juice, oil and black pepper to taste in a screwtop jar. Shake to combine.

5. Drizzle dressing over salad, and serve immediately.

Serves 8

Tuna Carpaccio in Witloof Leaves

Ingredients

200g/7oz fresh tuna or swordfish

4 witlof, leaves separated

1 red onion, diced

1 tablespoon capers, rinsed and drained

LIME AND HORSERADISH DRESSING:

2 tablespoons olive oil

2 tablespoons lime juice

1 tablespoon sherry or wine vinegar

1 teaspoon horseradish relish

Method

1. Using a sharp knife, cut fish into paper-thin slices. This will be easier to do if you place the fish in the freezer for 10 minutes before slicing, but take care to avoid freezing fish.

2. Divide fish among witlof leaves. Scatter each with diced onion and capers.

3. To make dressing, place oil, lime juice, vinegar and horseradish relish in a bowl. Whisk to combine.

4. Drizzle dressing over fish. Serve immediately with crostini or fresh crusty bread.

Serves 6

Scallop and Mango Sangchssajang

Ingredients

600g/21oz scallops

1 tablespoon cornflour

2 teaspoons brown sugar

2 teaspoons olive or peanut (groundnut) oil

2 shallots, thinly sliced

1 tablespoon grated fresh ginger

6 spears fresh asparagus, chopped

1/2 cup mirin or dry white wine

2 tablespoons lime or lemon juice

2 teaspoons fish sauce, optional

2 teaspoons reduced-salt soy sauce

1 small fresh red chilli, thinly sliced

1 mango, flesh diced

2 tablespoons shredded fresh sweet basil or coriander (cilantro)

2 cups cooked jasmine or calrose rice, hot

1 butter lettuce or radicchio, leaves separated

Method

1. Place scallops, cornflour and sugar in a plastic food bag. Toss gently to coat.

2. Heat 1 teaspoon of oil in a nonstick frying pan over a high heat. Add scallops. Stir-fry for 2–3 minutes or until scallops are just cooked. Remove scallops from pan. Set aside.

3. Add remaining oil to pan, and heat. Add shallots and ginger. Stir-fry for 1 minute or until soft. Add asparagus, mirin, lime juice, fish and soy sauces and chilli. Stir-fry for 4 minutes or until the asparagus is tender. Add mango and basil or coriander (cilantro). Toss to combine.

4. To serve, spoon rice into lettuce cups, then spoon in some of the scallop mixture. To eat, fold lettuce around scallops and eat in your hands.

Serves 4 as a light meal or 6 as an entreé

Witlof Speck Salad with Pipies and Mussels

Ingredients

400g/14oz pipis

400g/14oz mussels

1 onion, sliced

1 stalk celery, sliced

1 garlic clove, chopped

1 cup water or white wine

2 witlof, cut with leaves loose

4 slices of prosciutto, cooked under the grill and broken into small pieces

55mL/2fl oz virgin olive oil

1 tablespoon lemon juice

salt and pepper

MARINATED VEGETABLES:

1 carrot, peeled and sliced

$^{1}/_{2}$ onion, sliced in half

$^{1}/_{2}$ stalk celery

15 coriander seeds, cracked

salt and pepper

30mL/1fl oz sherry vinegar

1 cup water

Method

1. Put mussels and pipisin a large saucepan with onion, celery, garlic and water or wine. Cook until mussels and pipis have opened, stirring frequently to make sure they are cooked evenly. Allow to cool and remove from shells.

2. To prepare marinated vegetables put ingredients in a saucepan and boil for 2 minutes. Allow to cool down, then remove the cooking liquid

3. Mix all other ingredients together with the marinated vegetables. Add mussels and pipis to vegetable mixture, then put in refrigerator for 15 minutes until chilled. Serve with crispy bread or Italian Grissini.

Serves 4

Squid and Scallop Salad

Ingredients

1 red capsicum (pepper), seeded and halved

1 yellow or green capsicum (pepper), seeded and halved

2 squid tubes

255g/9oz scallops, roe removed

255g/9oz asparagus spears, cut into 5cm/2in pieces, blanched

1 Spanish onion, sliced

3 tablespoons fresh coriander (cilantro) leaves

1 bunch rocket or watercress

HERB AND BALSAMIC DRESSING:

1 tablespoon finely grated fresh ginger

1 tablespoon chopped fresh rosemary

1 clove garlic, crushed

$^1/_4$ cup olive oil

2 tablespoons lime juice

1 tablespoon balsamic or red wine vinegar

Method

1. To make dressing, put ginger, rosemary, garlic, oil, lime juice and vinegar in a screwtop jar and shake to combine. Set aside.

2. Preheat the barbecue to a high heat. Place red and yellow or green capsicum (pepper) halves, skin side down on lightly oiled barbecue grill and cook for 5–10 minutes or until skins are blistered and charred. Place peppers in a plastic food bag or paper bag and set aside until cool enough to handle. Remove skins and cut flesh into thin strips.

3. Cut squid tubes lengthwise and open out flat. Using a sharp knife cut parallel lines down the length of squid, taking care not to cut through the flesh. Make cuts in the opposite direction to form a diamond pattern. Cut into 5cm/2in squares.

4. Place squid and scallops on lightly oiled barbecue hotplate and cook, turning several times, for 3 minutes or until tender. Set aside to cool slightly.

5. Combine red and yellow or green capsicums (peppers), asparagus, onion and coriander. Line a large serving platter with rocket or watercress, top with vegetables, squid (calamari) and scallops. Drizzle with dressing and serve immediately.

Serves 4

Rock Lobster and Smoked Ocean Trout Salad

Ingredients

1 rock lobster, cooked

400g/14oz smoked ocean trout

1 continental cucumber

1 carrot

1 green zucchini (courgette)

1 yellow zucchini (courgette)

100g/3½ oz tatsoi leaves

1 bunch chives, snipped

DRESSING:

juice of 2 limes

1 tablespoon palm sugar

½ cup olive oil

salt and pepper

Method

1. Remove meat from tail of rock lobster, and slice finely and set aside. Alternatively ask your fishmonger to do this for you. Cut the smoked ocean trout into thin strips and set aside.

2. Slice cucumber in half lengthways and scoop out and discard the seeds. Slice on a mandoline or 'V-slicer' (or use a vegetable peeler) to make long, thin strips resembling fettuccine. Peel carrot and slice in the same way as cucumber. Slice zucchini lengthways into long thin strips.

3. Mix lobster, ocean trout, vegetables and tatsoi leaves together gently.

4. To make dressing, heat lime juice and add palm sugar to dissolve. Pour into a bowl and whisk in olive oil until the mixture is thick and the oil has emulsified with the lime juice. Season with salt and pepper and mix through salad ingredients.

5. Arrange salad on a platter and sprinkle with chives to serve.

Serves 6 – 8

Niçoise Salad

Ingredients

lettuce leaves of your choice

TUNA SALAD:

400g/14oz canned tuna, drained and flaked

115g/4oz canned artichoke hearts, drained and sliced (optional)

115g/4oz tasty cheese (mature Cheddar), cubed

4 hard-boiled eggs, sliced

2 potatoes, cooked and sliced

2 tomatoes, sliced

1 onion, sliced

225g/8oz green beans, cooked

45g/1 1/2 oz stuffed olives, sliced

NIÇOISE DRESSING:

1/4 cup olive oil

2 tablespoons vinegar

1 clove garlic, crushed

1/2 teaspoon Dijon mustard

freshly ground black pepper

Method

1. To make tuna salad, place tuna, artichokes, if using, cheese, eggs, potatoes, tomatoes, onion, beans and olives in a large bowl and toss to combine.

2. To make dressing, place oil, vinegar, garlic, mustard and black pepper to taste in a screwtop jar and shake well to combine. Spoon dressing over salad and toss lightly.

3. Line a large serving platter with lettuce leaves and top with salad. For a complete meal, serve with crusty fresh or toasted French bread. Some anchovies and shavings of Parmesan cheese are delicious additions to this dish.

Note: Always buy the form of the product that best fits your menu. Less expensive shredded or flaked tuna is the perfect choice for a salad such as this; it's cheaper in price because of appearance, not quality. Feta cheese makes a delicious and more gourmet alternative to tasty cheese (mature Cheddar).

Serves 6

Chargrilled Calamari and Bean Mash Salad

Ingredients

4 large calamari tubes, cleaned

85mL/3fl oz extra virgin olive oil

6 cloves garlic, crushed

3 small red chillies, finely sliced

2 tablespoons fresh oregano, chopped

1 sprig rosemary

2 x 285g/10oz cans cannellini beans, rinsed and drained

4 spring onions, finely sliced

2 tablespoons fresh flat-leaf parsley

2 tablespoons lemon juice

rocket leaves

Method

1. Slit each calamari tube along 1 side with a sharp knife, cut into large pieces and using a sharp knife score the underside in a diamond pattern but do not cut through. Put 30mL/1fl oz of olive oil, 3 cloves garlic, 2 red chillies and oregano in a bowl with the calamari pieces, cover and marinate in the refrigerator for 1 – 3 hours.

2. Put 55mL/2fl oz of oil, rosemary, 3 cloves garlic and 1 chilli in a small saucepan and heat gently until garlic starts to turn golden. Strain flavoured oil and set aside. Discard the ingredients used to flavour the oil.

3. Put beans in another saucepan and heat through. Transfer half beans to a food processor. In a slow steady stream, pour flavoured oil into beans with the motor running. Fold the remaining whole beans into the purée mixture. Set aside to keep warm.

4. Heat a chargrill pan until very hot, drain the excess oil from calamari and chargrill it over a very high heat for a couple of minutes or until just cooked.

5. Fold spring onions and parsley through the bean mixture, put a generous mound on each plate and top with calamari pieces. Drizzle with lemon juice and serve with rocket.

Serves 6

Chickpea and Trout Salad

Ingredients

1 bunch curly endive, leaves separated

1 bunch rocket

400g/14oz canned chickpeas, rinsed and drained

115g/4oz herbed goat's cheese, crumbled

1 onion, sliced

255g/9oz smoked trout, skin and bones removed, flesh flaked

2 tablespoons chopped fresh basil

1 red capsicum (pepper), halved, roasted, skin removed and sliced

HONEY LIME DRESSING:

$^1/_2$ cup natural yoghurt

1 tablespoon chopped fresh mint

1 tablespoon ground cumin

1 tablespoon honey

1 tablespoon lime juice

Method

1. Arrange endive and rocket on a serving platter. Top with chickpeas, goat's cheese, onion and trout. Sprinkle salad with basil and top with red capsicum (pepper).

2. To make dressing, place yoghurt, mint, cumin, honey and lime juice in a bowl and mix to combine. Drizzle dressing over salad and serve immediately.

Note: Chickpeas are slightly crunchy and give a nutty flavour to salads such as this as well as casseroles, soups and other savoury dishes. Dried chickpeas can be used rather than canned if you wish.To cook chickpeas, soak overnight in cold water. Drain. Place in a large saucepan, cover with cold water and bring to the boil over a medium heat. Reduce heat and simmer for 45–60 minutes or until chickpeas are tender. Drain and cool.

Serves 4

Asparagus and Salmon Salad

Ingredients

750g/1$^{2}/_{3}$ lb asparagus spears, trimmed

lettuce leaves of your choice

510g/18oz smoked salmon slices

LEMON YOGHURT SAUCE:

1 cup natural low-fat yoghurt

1 tablespoon finely grated lemon rind

1 tablespoon lemon juice

1 tablespoon chopped fresh dill

1 teaspoon ground cumin

Method

1. Boil, steam or microwave asparagus spears until tender. Drain, refresh under cold, running water, drain again and chill. Arrange lettuce leaves, asparagus spears and salmon on serving plates.

2. To make sauce, place yogurt, lemon rind, lemon juice, dill and cumin in a small bowl and mix to combine.

3. Spoon sauce over salad, and cover and chill until required.

Note: If fresh asparagus spears are unavailable, green beans or snow peas (mangetout) are good alternatives for this recipe.

Serves 4

Warm Barbecued Octopus and Potato Salad (opposite)

Ingredients

500g/1 lb baby octopus, cleaned

500g/1 lb pink-skinned potatoes (desiree, pontiac or pink fir), washed

rocket or mixed salad greens

2 Lebanese cucumbers, chopped

2 green onions, finely sliced

LIME AND CHILLI MARINADE:

2 tablespoons olive oil

juice of 1 lime or lemon

1 fresh red chilli, diced

1 clove garlic, crushed

TOMATO CONCASSE (optional):

4 plum tomatoes, diced

1/2 cup/25g chopped fresh coriander (cilantro)

1/2 red onion, diced

1/3 cup balsamic or sherry vinegar

1 tablespoon olive oil

1 tablespoon lemon juice

freshly ground black pepper

Method

1. To make marinade, place oil, lime juice, chilli and garlic in a bowl. Mix to combine. Cut octopus in half lengthwise; if very small, leave whole. Add to marinade. Marinate in the refrigerator overnight or at least 2 hours.

2. Boil or microwave potatoes until tender. Drain. Cool slightly. Cut into bite-sized chunks.

3. To make concasse, place tomatoes, coriander, onion, vinegar, oil, lemon juice and black pepper to taste in a bowl. Mix to combine.

4. Preheat a barbecue hotplate or char-grill pan to very hot. Line a serving platter with rocket leaves. Top with potatoes, cucumber and onions. Drain octopus. Cook on barbecue or in pan, turning frequently, for 3–5 minutes or until tentacles curl - take care not to overcook or octopus will be tough.

5. To serve, spoon hot octopus over prepared salad. Top with concasse, if using. Accompany with crusty bread.

Serves 6

Scallop and Prawn Salad

Ingredients

12 uncooked king prawns, shelled and deveined

500g/1 lb scallops

2 large onions, sliced

DRESSING:

2 teaspoons finely chopped fresh dill

2 teaspoons finely chopped fresh parsley

2 teaspoons finely chopped fresh chives

1 clove garlic, crushed

1 tablespoon lime juice

1 cup red wine vinegar

4 tablespoons vegetable oil

freshly ground black pepper

Method

1. Heat a fryingpan or barbecue hotplate and cook scallops, prawns and onions for 3 – 4 minutes. Allow to cool

2. Combine all ingredients for dressing, and mix well.

3. Place seafood and onion in a bowl and toss in dressing. serve immediately.

Serves 6

Prawn and Pawpaw Salad

Ingredients

2 teaspoons vegetable oil

2 teaspoons chilli paste (*sambal oelek*)

2 stalks fresh lemon grass, chopped, or 1 teaspoon dried lemon grass, soaked in hot water until soft

2 tablespoons shredded fresh ginger

500g/1 lb medium uncooked prawns, shelled and deveined

1/2 Chinese cabbage, shredded

4 red or golden shallots, chopped

1 pawpaw, peeled and sliced

55g/2oz watercress leaves

55g/2oz chopped roasted peanuts

30g/1oz fresh coriander (cilantro) leaves

LIME AND COCONUT DRESSING:

1 teaspoon brown sugar

3 tablespoons lime juice

2 tablespoons Thai fish sauce (*nam pla*)

1 tablespoon coconut vinegar

Method

1. Heat oil in a frying pan over a high heat, add chilli paste (*sambal oelek*), lemon grass and ginger and stir-fry for 1 minute. Add prawns and stir-fry for 2 minutes or until prawns change colour and are cooked through. Set aside to cool.

2. Arrange cabbage, shallots, pawpaw, watercress, peanuts, coriander (cilantro) and prawn mixture on a platter.

3. To make dressing, place sugar, lime juice, fish sauce and vinegar in a bowl and mix to combine. Drizzle dressing over salad and serve immediately.

Serves 4

Couscous Salad with Seafood and Fresh Mint

(opposite)

Ingredients

½ cup olive oil

55mL/2fl oz fresh lemon juice

1 large clove garlic, minced

1 teaspoon celery seeds

salt and pepper to taste

¼ teaspoon turmeric

¼ teaspoon cumin

2 cups boiling vegetable stock

500g/1 lb green king prawns, shelled, tail left on

200g/7oz small calamari rings

285g/10oz couscous

3 tomatoes, finely diced

2 stalks celery, finely sliced

6 spring onions, chopped

20 fresh mint leaves, finely sliced

Method

1. Whisk together olive oil, lemon juice, garlic and celery seeds until thick, then season with salt and pepper. Set aside.

2. Add turmeric and cumin to simmering stock and stir. Add prawns and calamari, and poach gently for 2 minutes or until prawns are orange, then remove from the stock.

3. Place couscous in a large bowl, then pour remaining spiced stock over it. Stir well and cover, then allow to stand until water is absorbed, about 10 minutes.

4. Fluff up couscous with a fork and add prawn and calamari mixture, diced tomatoes, celery, spring onions and mint. Add olive oil mixture and mix well.

Serves 6

Cold Marinated Mussel Salad

Ingredients

1 small carrot, diced finely

55g/2oz cauliflower, broken into florets

½ red capsicum (pepper), diced finely

½ onion, diced finely

pinch saffron

10 coriander seeds, cracked

1½cups water

45mL/1½ fl oz sherry vinegar

300g/10½ oz mussels meat, off the shell (equivalent approximately 1kg/2¼ lb mussels in shell, cooked mariniere style, see page 237)

handful mesclun salad mix

cherry tomatoes, quartered

3 tablespoons virgin olive oil

salt and pepper

Method

1. In a saucepan on high heat put water, carrot, cauliflower, capsicum, onion, saffron and coriander seeds.

2. Bring to the boil and add sherry vinegar

Remove from heat, and allow to cool down. When cold strain vegetables from cooking liquid and discard liquid.

4. In a large salad bowl, mix together mussels, mesclun salad mix, tomatoes, olive oil, vegetables and season to taste. Serve with fresh crusty bread.

Serves 4

Crab Salad with Tomato Dressing

Ingredients

2 large dressed crabs (about 250g/9oz crabmeat)

1 large bulb fennel, thinly sliced, and feathery top chopped and reserved to garnish

85g/3oz mixed salad leaves

1 tablespoon snipped fresh chives

and paprika or cayenne pepper to garnish

FOR THE DRESSING:

2 large tomatoes

5 tablespoons olive oil

1 tablespoon white wine vinegar

4 tablespoons single cream

1 teaspoon chopped fresh tarragon

Salt and black pepper

pinch of caster sugar

dash of Worcestershire sauce

5cm/2in piece cucumber, diced

Method

1. To make dressing, place tomatoes in a bowl and cover with boiling water. Leave for 30 seconds, then skin, deseed and cut into small dice. Whisk together the oil and vinegar in a bowl, then whisk in cream, tarragon and seasoning. Add sugar and Worcestershire sauce to taste, then stir in tomatoes and cucumber.

2. Mix together crabmeat and sliced fennel and stir in 4 tablespoons of dressing. Arrange the salad leaves together with crab mixture on plates. Spoon over remaining dressing, then sprinkle with chives, chopped fennel top and paprika or cayenne pepper.

Serves 4

Seared Scallop Salad

Ingredients

2 teaspoons sesame oil

2 cloves garlic, crushed

400g/14oz scallops, cleaned

4 rashers bacon, chopped

1 cos lettuce, leaves separated

55g/2oz croutons

fresh Parmesan cheese

MUSTARD DRESSING:

3 tablespoons mayonnaise

1 tablespoon olive oil

1 tablespoon vinegar

2 teaspoons Dijon mustard

Method

1. To make dressing, place mayonnaise, olive oil, vinegar and mustard in a bowl, mix to combine and set aside.

2. Heat sesame oil in a frying pan over a high heat, add garlic and scallops and cook, stirring, for 1 minute or until scallops just turn opaque. Remove scallop mixture from pan and set aside. Add bacon to pan and cook, stirring, for 4 minutes or until crisp. Remove bacon from pan and drain on absorbent kitchen paper.

3. Place lettuce leaves in a large salad bowl, add dressing and toss to coat. Add bacon, croutons and shavings of Parmesan cheese and toss to combine. Spoon scallop mixture over salad and serve.

Serves 4-6

Thai Squid Salad

Ingredients

3 squid tubes, cleaned

200g/7oz green beans, sliced lengthwise

2 tomatoes, cut into wedges

1 small green pawpaw, peeled, seeded and shredded

4 spring onions, sliced

30g/1oz fresh mint leaves

30g/1oz fresh coriander (cilantro) leaves

1 fresh red chilli, chopped

LIME DRESSING:

2 teaspoons brown sugar

3 tablespoons lime juice

1 tablespoon Thai fish sauce (*nam pla*)

Method

1. Using a sharp knife, make a single cut down the length of each squid tube and open out. Cut parallel lines down the length of squid, taking care not to cut through the flesh. Make more cuts in the oppos te direction to form a diamond pattern.

2. Heat a nonstick chargrill or frying pan over a high heat, add squid and cook for 1 – 2 minutes each side or until tender. Remove from pan and cut into thin strips.

3. Place squid, beans, tomatoes, pawpaw, spring onions, mint, coriander and chilli in a serving bowl.

4. To make dressing, place sugar, lime juice and fish sauce in a screwtop jar and shake well. Drizzle over salad and toss to combine. Cover and stand for 20 minutes before serving.

Serving suggestion: Serve this salad with soy rice noodles. Boil 370g/13oz fresh rice noodles, drain and sprinkle with a little reduced-salt soy sauce. Scatter with toasted sesame seeds and toss to combine with salad.

Serves 4

Tarragon Seafood Salad

Ingredients

4 tablespoons chopped fresh tarragon

2 tablespoons lime juice

3 teaspoons grated lime rind

1 fresh red chilli, chopped

2 teaspoons olive oil

freshly ground black pepper

500g/1 lb uncooked lobster tail, flesh removed from shell and cut into large pieces or 500g/1 lb firm white fish fillets, cut into large pieces

225g/8oz snow pea (mangetout) sprouts or watercress

1 cucumber, sliced into ribbons

2 carrots, sliced into ribbons

1 red capsicum (bell pepper), cut into thin strips

Method

1. Place tarragon, lime juice, lime rind, chilli, oil and black pepper to taste in a bowl and mix to combine. Add lobster, toss to coat and set aside to marinate for 15 minutes.

2. Make cucumber and carrot ribbons, use a vegetable peeler to remove strips lengthwise from the cucumber or carrot. Arrange snow pea sprouts or watercress, cucumber, carrot and red capsicum (bell pepper) on a large serving platter and set aside.

3. Heat a chargrill or frying pan over a high heat, add lobster mixture and cook, turning frequently, for 2 minutes or until lobster is tender. Arrange lobster over salad, spoon over pan juices and serve immediately.

Note: This salad is also delicious made with prawns instead of lobster. If using prawns, shell and devein them before marinating.

Serves 4

Seafood Salad

Ingredients

370g/13oz calamari rings

1 tablespoon olive oil

370g/13oz uncooked medium prawns, peeled and deveined

1 clove garlic, crushed

1 bunch spinach

1 Spanish onion, sliced

1 red capsicum (pepper), cut into strips

225g/8oz snow peas (mangetout), trimmed

2 tablespoons fresh mint leaves

30g/1oz peanuts, finely chopped

CHILLI DRESSING:

2 tablespoons sweet chilli sauce

1 tablespoon soy sauce

1 tablespoon lime juice

1 tablespoon vegetable oil

Method

1. Place calamari on absorbent kitchen paper and pat dry.

2. Heat oil in a frying pan over a medium heat, add prawns and garlic and stir-fry for 2 minutes. Add squid (calamari) and stir-fry for 2 minutes more. Set aside to cool.

3. Arrange spinach, onion, red capsicum (pepper), snow peas (mangetout), mint and nuts in a bowl or on a serving platter. Top with seafood mixture.

4. To make dressing, place chilli sauce, soy sauce, lime juice and oil in a bowl and mix to combine. Spoon dressing over salad and chill before serving with fresh crusty bread or rolls.

Serves 4

Avocado Seafood

Ingredients

6 baby octopus

500g/1 lb cooked prawns, tails intact

3 ripe avocados

6 sprigs oregano

DRESSING:

1/3 cup olive oil

2 tablespoons lemon juice

1 hard-boiled egg, finely chopped

1 tablespoon fresh oregano, chopped

2 cloves garlic, crushed

Method

1. Remove heads from octopus just below eye level. Wash well. Drop octopus into simmering water, cook until just opaque, drain and rinse under cold water. Cut octopus into bite size pieces. Combine with dressing, which is made by combining all ingredients and mixing well. Marinate in the refrigerator overnight.

2. Add prawns to octopus. Halve avocados, remove seeds. Pile seafood on top of avocado halves. Garnish sprigs of oregano.

Serves 6

Prawn and Pineapple Salad

Ingredients

10 water chestnuts, drained and chopped

1 tablespoon grated green ginger

225g/8oz canned sliced pineapple, drained and cut into chunks

500g/1 lb cooked prawns, shelled

8 lettuce leaves, shaped like cups

3 spring onions, sliced

1 tablespoon sesame seeds, toasted lightly

DRESSING:

1 tablespoon lemon juice
2 tablespoons white wine vinegar
1 tablespoon Dijon mustard
$^{1}/_{4}$ cup olive oil
2 tablepoons sesame oil

Method

1. In a bowl place chopped water chestnuts, ginger, pineapple and prawns.

2. To make dressing, whisk lemon juice, vinegar and mustard together, then gradually adding oils, whisking all the time until dressing is thickened.

3. Add dressing to chestnut mixture and toss together lightly.

4. Arrange the salad lettuce cups and garnish with spring onion and sesame seeds.

Serves 4

Mixed Shellfish and Potato Salad

Ingredients

750g/1 2/3 lb waxy potatoes, unpeeled

salt

4 small cooked beetroot, diced

1 head fennel, finely sliced, plus feathery top, chopped

1kg/2 1/4 lb mussels

500g/1 lb cockles

1 1/5 cups dry white wine or dry cider

1 shallot, finely chopped

4 spring onions, finely sliced

3 tablespoon chopped fresh parsley

DRESSING:

5 tablespoon olive oil

1 1/2 tablespoon cider vinegar

1/2 teaspoon English mustard

salt and pepper to taste

Method

1. To make dressing, whisk together oil, vinegar, mustard and season to taste. Boil potatoes in salted water for 15 minutes or until tender, then drain. Cool for 30 minutes, then peel and slice. Place in a bowl and toss with half the dressing. Toss beetroot and fennel with the rest of dressing.

2. Scrub mussels and cockles under cold, running water, pulling away any beards from mussels. Discard any shellfish that are open or damaged. Place wine or cider and shallot in a large saucepan and bring to the boil. Simmer for 2 minutes, then add shellfish. Cover and cook briskly for 3–5 minutes, shaking the pan often, or until opened. Discard any that remain closed. Reserve the pan juices, set aside a few mussels in their shells and shell the rest.

3. Boil the pan juices for 5 minutes or until reduced to 1–2 tablespoons. Strain over potatoes. Add shellfish, spring onions and parsley, then toss. Serve with the beetroot and fennel salad and garnish with fennel tops and mussels in their shells.

Serves 4

Honeyed Squid Salad

Ingredients

6 small squid, cleaned and sliced into rings or 370g/13oz frozen squid rings instead.

1/2 cup flour

olive oil for shallow-frying

lettuce leaves of your choice

225g/8oz cherry tomatoes, halved

1 onion, thinly sliced

HONEY ORANGE DRESSING:

1/4 cup olive oil

1 tablespoon orange juice

1 tablespoon vinegar

1 teaspoon honey

1 clove garlic, crushed

1/2 teaspoon mild mustard

freshly ground black pepper

Method

1. To make dressing, place oil, orange juice, vinegar, honey, garlic, mustard and black pepper to taste in a screwtop jar and shake well to combine.

2. Dry squid rings on absorbent kitchen paper. Toss in flour and shake off excess. Heat oil in a frying pan over a medium heat, add squid and stir-fry for 1–2 minutes or until golden. Drain on absorbent kitchen paper.

3. Place lettuce leaves, tomatoes and onion in a bowl and toss. Divide lettuce mixture between serving plates, top with hot squid and drizzle with dressing. Serve immediately.

Serves 4

Salad of Lobster with Raspberries

(opposite)

Ingredients

2 lobster tails, cooked and shells removed

1 small radicchio, leaves separated

1 small mignonette lettuce, leaves separated

100g/3 1/2 oz snow pea sprouts or watercress

1 orange, segmented

225g/8oz strawberries, halved

DRESSING:

115g/4oz fresh or frozen raspberries

2 tablespoons raspberry vinegar

2 tablespoons vegetable oil

1 teaspoon finely chopped fresh mint

1 tablespoon sugar

Method

1. Cut lobster tails into 1cm/1/2in medallions and set aside.

2. Arrange radicchio, mignonette, sprouts or watercress, lobster, orange segments and strawberries on a serving platter, and refrigerate until required.

3. To make dressing, place raspberries in a food processor or blender and process until puréed. Push through a sieve to remove seeds. Combine raspberry purée with vinegar, oil, mint and sugar. Mix well to combine, pour over salad and serve immediately.

Serves 4

Green Mussel Salad

Ingredients

$1^1/_2$ kg/$3^1/_3$ lb mussels in their shells

5 tablespoons water

$^1/_2$ cup extra virgin olive oil

2 tablespoons white wine vinegar

2 teaspoons capers, well drained

2 tablespoons finely chopped Spanish onion

$^1/_2$ clove garlic, finely chopped

2 tablespoons chopped fresh parsley

1 teaspoon paprika

small pinch cayenne pepper

salt

Method

1. Clean mussels and discard any that are open. In a large saucepan, put mussels with water. Cover pan and boil for 4–5 minutes, shaking pan occasionally or until shells open. Drain mussels and discard any that remain closed. Remove mussels from shells and discard shells.

2. In a bowl, mix together remaining ingredients. Stir in mussels, cover and refrigerate overnight. Return to room temperature before serving.

Serves 4

Tuna and Lemon Fettuccine Salad

Ingredients

500g/1 lb fettuccine

400g/14oz canned tuna in spring water, drained and flaked

200g/7oz rocket leaves, roughly chopped

145g/5oz reduced-fat feta cheese, chopped

1 tablespoon chopped fresh dill

$^{1}/_{4}$ cup lemon juice

freshly ground black pepper

Method

1. Cook fettuccine in boiling water in a large saucepan following packet directions. Drain and return pasta to saucepan.

2. Place the saucepan over a low heat, and add tuna, rocket, cheese, dill, lemon juice and black pepper to taste. Toss to combine, and serve immediately.

Serves 4

sushi and sashimi

EQUIPMENT

This is a basic set of utensils for making sushi.

A RICE-COOLING TUB (Hangiri)

is used for cooling the vinegared rice, giving it the perfect texture and gloss. It is made of cypress bound with copper hoops, but any wooden or plastic vessel can be used instead.

A SPATULA (Shamoji)

is used to turn and spread sushi rice while cooling it. Traditionally the spatula is a symbol of the housewife's position in the household. You can use an ordinary spoon instead, wooden or plastic.

A FAN (Uchiwa)

is used to drive off moisture and encourage evaporation to get the right texture and flavour of sushi rice. Traditionally this fan is made of bamboo ribs covered with either paper or silk. If fan isn't available, use a piece of cardboard or a magazine instead.

BOWL

A large bowl with a lid is necessary to store cooked sushi rice in order to keep it warm while making your sushi.

CHOPPING BOARD (Manaita)

This is a must traditionally chopping boards are made of wood, but today many people prefer chopping boards made of rubber or resin. These are easier to keep clean.

CHOPSTICKS (Saibashi)

Basically there are two types of chopsticks. Long chopsticks for cooking, often made from metal, are handy once their use is mastered, for picking things up and shorter chopsticks for eating.

TWEEZERS

Tweezers are used to remove small bones from fish. Larger, straight-ended tweezers are better than the smaller variety commonly found in the bathroom and can be obtained from fish markets or specialty stores.

ROLLING MAT (Makisu)

Made of bamboo woven together with cotton string, a rolling is used to make rolled sushi.

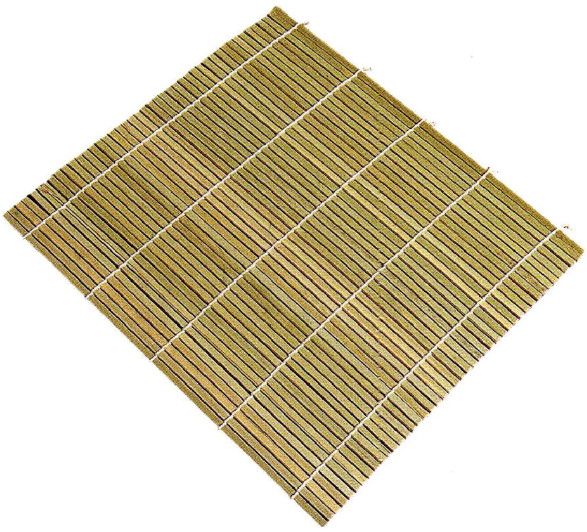

KNIVES

The only way to get nicely cut surfaces is to use steel knives of good quality. Use a whetstones to sharpen the blades yourself. Good Japanese knives are an outgrowth of forging the Japanese sword, which is world famous for its sharpness. The knives are a chef's most valuable possession, and sushi chefs keep a wet cloth near by, frequently wiping the blades to keep their knives clean as they work. Here are the basic types:

Cleaver (Deba-bocho)

A clever is a wide heavy knife with a triangular-shaped blade capable of cutting bone.

Vegetable knife (Nakiri-bocho)

A vegetable knife is lighter than a cleaver. Its blade is rectangular in shape.

Fish knife (Sashimi-bocho)

A fish knife is long and slender. The pointed type is most popular in Osaka, and the blunt-ended type is most popular in Tokyo. A fish knife is excellent for filleting and slicing fish, and also for slicing rolled sushi.

Ingredients

VINEGAR

Sugared water or any alcoholic beverage, allowed to stand long enough, naturally sours and becomes vinegar. The origin of the word is French and comes from *vin* (wine) and *aigre* (sour). In Japan vinegar is made from rice, the grain from which sake is brewed. With the power to alter proteins, vinegar destroys bacteria. Adding sugar to sushi rice prevents the tartness of vinegar coming through too strongly.

SOY SAUCE

Soy sauce is popular all over the world, used under many different names: all flavour, meat sauce, all purpose seasoning, etc. Japanese soy sauce, rather than the darker and richer Chinese variety, is the one for sushi lovers. Soy sauce is highly recommended as a naturally fermented food, superior to salt, sugar or synthetic seasonings. It is essential to most traditional Japanese foods, including sushi, tempura, sukiyaki and noodles.

Once opened, soy sauce should be stored in a cool, dark and dry place or refrigerated.

To tell good soy sauce from bad, use the following guidelines:

Aroma
A good soy sauce never produces an unpleasant smell, no matter how deeply you inhale.

Colour
When a small quantity is poured into a white dish, good soy sauce looks reddish.

Clarity
Good soy sauce is perfectly translucent. Sunlight passing through it gives it a lovely glow.

NORI (seaweed)

After harvesting, seaweed is dried, toasted and sold in packaged in standard size sheets (19X21cm/7½X8½in). Once the sealed cellophane or plastic bag has been opened, nori should be eaten at once. If not it should be stored in a sealed container in a dry, cool, dark place to preserve its crispiness. Nori is particularly rich in vitamins A, B12 and D.

Nori belts are used on nigiri-sushi when the topping being used is likely to slip off the rice, such as omelette and tofu.

Simply cut a strip of nori about 1cm/½in wide and wrap it around the topping and rice to secure it.

SAKE

Sake is a colourless brewed alcoholic beverage made from rice that is legally defined as a rice beer. Its bouquet is somewhat earthy, with subtle undertones; it has a slightly sweet initial taste, followed by a dry aftertaste. Sake should be stored in a cool, dark place prior to opening, then in the refrigerator after opening. Very popular in Japan, it is the traditional drink served before eating sushi, and should be served warm.

MIRIN

Mirin is know as sweet sake, and is generally only used for seasoning. If unavailable, sweet sherry makes a suitable substitute.

DAIKON RADISH

daikon radish is a Japanese white radish, available fresh in Asian foodshops, in sizes ranging from 15cm/6in to 90cm/3ft. It may be refrigerated for several weeks. Cut into very fine slivers, it is commonly eaten with sashimi and can be used as a substitute for nori seaweed. When it is minced, it can be added to soy sauce for a different texture and flavour.

TOFU

Tofu is a custard-like cake of soya-bean curd, about 8cm/3in square. Sold fresh in supermarkets, it will keep for several days if refrigerated and left in fresh water. Often it is used in nigiri-sushi as a substitute for sushi rice, or as a topping on the rice.

SUSHI RICE

When it comes to sushi, the rice is as important as the fish, and it takes years of training to learn how to make perfect sushi rice. There are different ways of doing it, but by following the directions on page 78 you will have a universally accepted and uncomplicated method of making the rice.

SESAME SEEDS

White sesame seeds are roasted and used as an aromatic seasoning, while black seeds are used mostly as a garnish.

PICKLED GINGER (Gari or Shoga)

Ginger is used to cleanse the palate between bites of sushi. It does not take a lot of ginger to cleanse the palate, so a small pile should be enough for several rolls. Pickled ginger can be bought in Asian food stores, but if you wish to make your own, try this recipe.

Ingredients

225g/8oz ginger root

85ml/3fl oz rice vinegar

2 tablespoons mirin

2 tablespoons sake

5 teaspoons sugar

Method

1. Scrub the ginger root under running water as you would a potato for baking. Blanch in boiling water for minute and drain. Slice ginger very finely.

2. Combine rice vinegar, mirin, sake, and sugar in a small saucepan. Bring to a boil, stirring until sugar has dissolved. Cool.

3. Place ginger into a sterilised jar and pour cooled vinegar over the ginger. Cover and keep 3 - 4 days before using. It will keep refrigerated for up to 1 month. The pale pink colour develops as it ages, however, you may want to add a small amount of red food colouring.

Ingredients (continued)

WASABI

Grown only in Japan, wasabi horseradish, when grated finely, is a pungent, refreshing pulp that removes unpleasant fishiness. Fresh wasabi is very expensive and difficult to obtain, so the best alternative is the powdered variety. Mix it with water to get a firm consistency. The wasabi purchased in tubes tends too be to strong and lacking that real wasabi flavour.

TEZU

Tezu is a bowl of half sushi vinegar and half water, used to make it easier to handle sushi rice and toppings.

Mayonnaise

Mayonnaise is not extensively used in sushi cooking, with the exception of California Rolls.

Instead of using the standard commercially-made egg mayonnaise, try this homemade variety with a slight Japanese influence.

Ingredients

3 egg yolks

1/2 teaspoon lemon juice

1 cup/250ml/8fl oz vegetable oil

50g/1 1/2 oz white miso

salt to taste

sprinkle of white pepper

a pinch of grated yuzu*, lime, or lemon peel

*Yuzu is a Japanese orange used only for its rind. Kaffir lime used in Thai or Malaysian food is an alternative, as is lemon or lime rind.

Method

1. In a bowl, beat egg yolks and lemon juice with a wooden spoon.

2. Continue to beat, adding the vegetable oil a few drops at a time until the mixture begins to emulsify. Keep on adding rest of oil, then stir in the miso and the seasonings.

Refrigerate before using.

Preparing Sushi Rice

Rice cooked for sushi should be slightly harder in texture than rice used for other dishes. The rice you use should be short-grained rice.

You will need approximately one cup of cooked rice for each roll. It is easier to make too much rice than too little. Every recipe for sushi rice is different, but they all work. You might find a recipe on your bottle of rice vinegar, on the bag of rice or on the package of nori.

Most recipes call for rinsing the raw rice until the water runs clear, but it can be avoided. The reason it is rinsed first is to remove talc from the rice. Today, most rice seems to be coated with a type of cereal starch, rather than talc, so rinsing may be omitted.

Most recipes also suggest letting the rinsed rice drain in a colander, or zaru, for 30 - 60 minutes. It's up to you.

Ingredients

4 cups short grain rice

4 cups water

Sushi vinegar:

$^1/_2$ cup rice vinegar

4 tablesoop sugar

2 teaspoon salt

1 teaspoon soy sauce

Method

1. Wash rice until water is clear. Combine rice and water in a sauce pan and set aside for 30 minutes. Bring rice and water to boil. Reduce heat to very low and simmer for 10 minutes. Turn off heat and leave rice for 20 minutes to steam.

2. Make sushi vinegar by mixing all ingredients in a saucepan over heat until dissolved.

3. Spread rice on a baking tray, then sprinkle sushi vinegar over rice and mix it as if cutting. Use a fan to cool rice until it reaches room temperature.

Note: One of the important criteria of well-made sushi is that the rice does not break when you pick it up.

Tips:

1. Most beginners hold too much rice . Hold less than you think you need.

2. Most beginners put too much water on their hands. Use only a small amount.

Making Nigiri Sushi

1. Prepare the *tezu*, which consists of half water, half sushi vinegar. Moisten fingers and palms with the *tezu*.

2. Pick up a piece of fish in one hand, and with the other a small handful of prepared sushirice. Gently squeeze the rice to form a block. To prepare sushi rice, use recipe on page 81.

3. With the piece of fish lying in the palm of your hand, spread a small amount of wasabi along the fish.

4. With the piece of fish still in your palm, place rice on top of the fish. Use your thumb to press down slightly on the rice, making a small depression.

5. Using the forefinger of your other hand, press down on the rice, causing it to flatten.

6. Turn the sushi over (fish side up), and using your thumb and middle finger, squeeze the rice together.

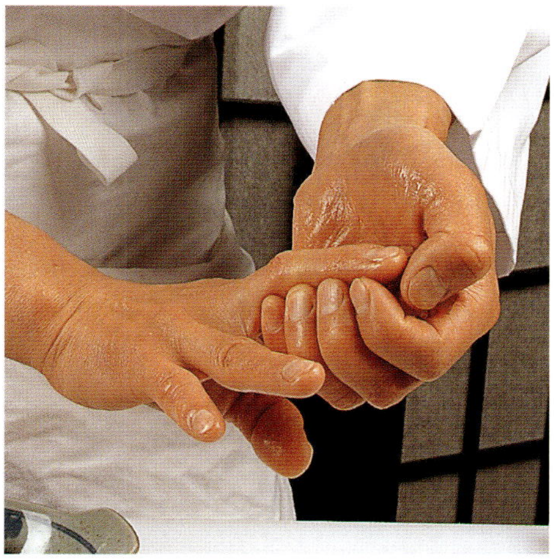

7. Position fingers and hand as shown above, covering the fish and rice. Gently squeeze around the sushi. Repeat steps 5 - 7 twice more.

8. You should now have a piece of finished sushi, with the fish covering the firm rice.

Nigiri Sushi with Prawns (Ebi)

Ingredients

10 thin bamboo skewers (15cm/5in long)

2 cups water

10 green king prawns

1 teaspoon salt

1 teaspoon vinegar

300g/10½ oz sushi rice

2 teaspoons wasabi paste

vinegar water or tezu

(use 1 cup water and 1 cup vinegar)

Method

1. Insert a bamboo skewer through each prawn to prevent curling.

2. Use a saucepan holding 2 cups of water. Into the saucepan put water, and bring to the boil. Add salt and vinegar, then drop the prawns into the water and simmer for 2–3 minutes. Scoop out prawns and drop them into iced water. Refresh with cold water if necessary to ensure prawns are well chilled.

3. Twist skewer to remove each prawn. Then shell prawns removing the legs and head, but leave the tip of the tail intact. To remove the vein, slice lengthwise along the back and pull vein out. Insert the knife along the leg side of each prawn and open like a butterfly.

4. Soak prawns in salted water for 20 minutes. Then transfer into a bowl of vinegar water and soak for further 20 minutes.

8. Proceed to make nigiri-sushi as described on pages 82–83.

Makes 10 sushi

Nigiri Sushi with Salmon (sake)

Ingredients

300g/10½ oz salmon fillet

300g/10½ oz sushi rice

1 tablespoon wasabi

Method

1. Pick up a piece of thinly sliced salmon fillet with your left hand between thumb and index finger. (see pages 82–83)

2. Shape about 15g/½ oz of sushi rice (a bit smaller than golf ball).

3. Place a dab of wasabi in centre of the salmon with your index finger.

4. Put rice onto salmon.

5. Press the rice with your left thumb, it will leave a small depression in the ball.

6. Press the upper and bottom of the rice between the index finger and thumb of your right hand.

7. Press the surface of the rice with your right index finger.

8. Close the left hand gently then turn towards to right.

9. Now the topping should face upward. Then place index and middle finger on the topping.

10. Close your left hand then lift up gently.

11. Turn clockwise with your right index finger and thumb.

12. Press both sides then repeat steps 7–11, 2 or 3 times

Makes 20 sushi

Nigiri Sushi with Tuna (Maguru)

Ingredients

300g/$10\frac{1}{2}$ oz tuna fillet

300g/$10\frac{1}{2}$ oz sushi rice

1 tablespoon wasabi

Instructions

Proceed to make nigiri-sushi as described on pages 82 - 83.

Note: There are several different varieties of tuna available both at the fish market and also to the fisher.

The 4 recommended types of tuna are:

1. Bluefin tuna is considered by most Japanese to be the superior fish of the tuna family.

2. Bigeye tuna is also highly regarded, only exceeded in price on the Japanese markets by bluefin tuna.

3. Yellowfin tuna is an extremely important and widely resourced tropical tuna. It is air freighted, fresh chilled, to Japan, but increasing quantities are now absorbed by local sashimi markets.

4 Albacore is well regarded for sashimi, but quite high in calories. It is often referred to as the 'chicken of the sea' with its slight chicken flavour when cooked.

Makes 20 sushi

Nigiri Sushi with Sea Eel (Anago)

(opposite)

Ingredients

1 4/5 cups water

225g/8oz seawater eel fillet

3 tablespoons sugar

3 tablespoons soy sauce

225g/8oz sushi rice

1 tablespoon wasabi

20 nori belts

Method

1. Bring water to the boil, place eel in and allow to cook for about 1 minute, then refresh in cold water.

2. Add sugar and soy sauce to the boiling water.

3. Place eel back into the boiling water. Cook for 20 minutes and then remove from the heat.

4. Allow to cool and then proceed to make nigiri sushi as described on pages 82–83.

5. Wrap nigiri sushi with nori belt.

Makes 15 - 20 sushi

Nigiri Sushi with Freshwater Eel (Unagi) (opposite)

Ingredients

$^1/_2$ cup soy sauce

2 tablespoons sugar

1 cup mirin

1 pre-cooked *unagi* eel

225g/8oz sushi rice

1 tablespoon wasabi

20 nori belts

Instructions

1. Combine soy sauce, sugar and mirin in a saucepan. Bring to the boil and reduce until half remains.

2. Thinly slice eel and grill for 2 minutes, basting with the reduced soy sauce mixture.

3. Proceed to make nigiri sushi as described on pages 82–83.

4. Wrap nigiri sushi with nori belt.

Note: A fresh Unagi eel is very hard to obtain, and even harder to prepare. Asian supermarkets or a good fishmonger should have supplies of prepared Unagi eel.

Makes 15 - 20 sushi

Chirashi Sushi

Suggestions for toppings

Tuna

Prawns

Omelette

Cuttlefish

Salmon

Unagi eel

Yellowtail

Bonito

Avocado

Tofu

Crab

Vegetables

- The easiest type of sushi to make, made in all Japanese kitchens, is "*chirashi* sushi" or scattered sushi. *Chirashi* sushi is simply sushi rice with other ingredients mixed in or placed on the rice.
- *Chirashi* sushi without any seafood often makes its appearance in lunch boxes. It's taken on picnics and often sold on railway station platforms. "Station lunches" are not exclusively *chirashi* sushi but many are. Stations are known for their type of food as well as for their unique lunch containers in which they package their lunches.
- Again, the variations of this type of sushi are almost limitless. The rice can also be seasoned with a range of interesting ingredients such as chopped vegetables, sesame seeds, tofu pieces, chopped fresh and pickled ginger, crumbled nori and a variety of sauces.

Tofu Sushi

Ingredients

300g/10½ oz tofu (substitute for sushi rice)

grated ginger

chopped shallot

1 teaspoon soy sauce

assortment of fish

meat and vegetables

15–20 nori belts

Instructions

1. Cut the tofu into 1in x ½in pieces

2. Mix ginger, shallot and soy sauce together.

3. Place topping onto tofu and tie with nori belt. Put a little mixed ginger on top then serve. As the garnish already contains soy, bowls of soy and wasabi are not necessary

Makes 20 sushi

Making Thin Sushi Rolls

1. Cut 1 nori sheet in half lengthwise. Use two pieces for making the sushi rolls. Place nori shiny side down onto the mat. Moisten your hands with some *tezu*.

2. Take a handful of rice from the rice-cooling tub. Spread rice over nori, taking care to do so evenly.

3. With your forefinger, spread the desired amount of wasabi across rice, starting at one end and spreading it across the middle to the other end.

4. Place tuna strips along the centre of rice, on top of wasabi. Lift the edge of the bamboo mat.

5. With fingers of both hands, hold onto the mat and the filling. Wrap the mat and nori over the filling, ensure that all ingredients are evenly pressed.

6. Continue rolling, but apply a little more pressure to compact rice. If needed, repeat the last step to ensure rice is pressed firmly and evenly along the roll.

7. Remove roll from the mat, and place on a cutting board. Cut roll in half.

8. Generally, allow 6 pieces per roll, so lie the 2 halves next to each other and cut into thirds.

Cucumber Rolls (Kappamaki)

(opposite)

Ingredients

2 sheets nori (cut in half)

1 cup sushi rice

4 pieces cucumber, each cut into strips

$\frac{1}{2}$ x 1 x 7$\frac{1}{2}$cm ($\frac{1}{4}$ x $\frac{1}{4}$ x 3in)

1 teaspoon wasabi

Method

Proceed to make cucumber rolls as described on pages 92–93.

Note: Variations other than those described here are possible.

Ingredients such as fresh salmon, smoked salmon, prawns, avocado, minced tuna with chilli, omelette and umeboshi plums are tasty alternatives.

Makes 24 piece

Tuna Rolls (Tekkamaki)

(opposite)

Ingredients

2 nori sheets (cut in half)

1 cup sushi rice

4 pieces tuna, each cut into strips

$\frac{1}{2}$ x 1 x 7$\frac{1}{2}$ cm ($\frac{1}{4}$ x $\frac{1}{4}$ x 3in)

1 teaspoon wasabi

Instructions

Proceed to make tuna rolls as described on pages 92–93.

Makes 24 pieces

Making Thick Sushi Rolls

1. Lay 1 sheet of nori shiny side down onto the bamboo rolling mat, moisten your hands with some *tezu* and take a handful of sushi rice.

2. Spread rice evenly over the surface of nori.

3. Add the desired amount of wasabi along the middle of rice.

4. Add a little Japanese mayonnaise as well.

5. Add the fillings you wish to use, placing them in the middle and on top of wasabi and mayonnaise.

6. Start rolling the mat up over the fillings, stopping when you get to about $2^{1}/_{2}$cm/1in away from the end of nori.

7. Lift the mat up and roll forward again to join the edges of nori together, while at the same time applying a small amount of pressure to make roll firm.

8. Using a sharp knife, cut the completed rolls in half, then place the halves next to each other and cut into thirds. Each roll will provide 6 pieces.

California Roll (Ura Makisushi)

(opposite)

Ingredients

4 medium cooked prawns or seafood sticks

4 nori sheets

3 cups sushi rice

1 tablespoon wasabi

45g/1½oz Japanese mayonnaise

4–8 coral lettuce leaves

1 ripe avocado, peeled, seeded and sliced

1 cucumber, cut into thin slices

8 teaspoons flying fish roe

Method

1. Shell and de-vein prawns and slice in half lengthways.

2. Proceed to make California Rolls as described on pages 96–97.

Variations: Wash 1 large carrot, cut in thick strips and blanch. In salt water, blanch 85g/3oz English spinach, rinse in cold water, drain and shake dry. Cut 85g/3oz fresh salmon fillet in finger thick slices and marinate in mirin. Prepare the California Roll as described on pages 96–97.

Makes 16 pieces

Dynamite Roll (Spicy Tuna)

Ingredients

145g/5oz tuna fillet, minced

1 teaspoon chilli bean sauce (or Korean Kimchee to substitute)

30g/1oz shallots, chopped

4 nori sheets

1 tablespoon wasabi

3 cups sushi rice

Method

1. Combine tuna, chilli bean sauce and shallots.

2. Proceed to make rolls as described on pages 96–97.

Makes 16 pieces

Making Inside Out Rolls

1. Have a nori sheet lying on a bamboo rolling mat, and pick up a small handful of sushi rice.

2. Spread rice evenly over the nori. Then take nori and rice off the board and place on a damp cloth.

3. With nori and rice on the damp cloth, spread the desired amount of wasabi down the centre of nori.

4. Add ingredients along the centre of nori.

5. Start rolling the mat up over the filling, stopping when you get to about 2½cm/ 1in away from the end of nori.

6. Lift the mat up and roll forward again to join the edges of nori together, while at the same time applying a small amount of pressure to firm roll.

7. Remove the completed roll from the mat and place onto a plate. Gradually spoon roe around roll until there is a sufficient coating of roe on rice.

8. Using a sharp knife, cut the completed rolls in half, place the halves next to each other and cut into thirds. Each roll will provide 6 pieces.

Inside-out Rolls (Sakamaki)

Ingredients

200g/7oz salmon fillet

1 ripe avocado

1 cucumber

4 nori sheets

3 cups sushi rice

8 teaspoons flying fish roe

1 tablespoon wasabi

Instructions

1. Prepare the fillings for rolls. Slice salmon, avocado and cucumber into suitable lengths.

2. Proceed to make inside-out rolls as described on page 100–101.

Note: Fillings can be varied depending on seasonal availability of ingredients. Avocado is not always available, so choose whatever suits your taste. Instead of flying fish roe on the outside of the roll, sesame seeds, salmon roe or dried bonito flakes make tasty alternatives.

Makes 16 pieces

sushi & sashimi

Temaki Sushi

Originally *temaki* sushi was a meal for busy chefs. Having the ingredients on hand but no time to make sushi for themselves, they created this 'hand-roll sushi'. *Temaki* offers one more sushi variation in a cone shape. *Temaki* offers a good way to experiment with ingredients, such as cooked chicken and raw or rare beef, perhaps seasoned with flavoursome sauces. *Temaki* are quick and easy to prepare and taste delicious, even with an inexpensive filling.

- If you cannot buy roasted nori sheets, you can roast them yourself. Lightly toast 1 side of the sheet of nori for about 30 seconds over a gas flame. Toasting both sides seems to diminish the taste. Or toast them in a frying pan without oil on low heat until the aroma comes out. The nori will be crisp and have a dark green colour after cooking.
- Leftover roasted nori sheets can be chopped and used as a seasoning, or just to nibble on.
- If you make *temaki* sushi with soft or semi-liquid ingredients, it is easier with the rice at the bottom and the filling above it.
- In Japan the fresh sprouts of the daikon radish are popular ingredients for *temaki* and *maki* sushi. They resemble large mustard and cress, but are much and spicier. They go well with Omelette Sushi. Daikon sprouts are available in Asian supermarkets and greengrocers. You can grow them as well at home from the seeds of the daikon radish.

Small *temaki* sushi are perfect as an appetiser, because they are easy to eat as fingerfood.

Ingredients

10 nori sheets, halved

500g/1 lb sushi rice

wasabi

Method

Proceed to make temaki sushi as described on pages 106–107.

Suggestions for Fillings

Tuna slices

Spicy tuna (see page 98)

Tempura prawns

Teriyaki chicken

Cooked prawns

Crab sticks

Unagi eel fillets

Pickled whiting or yellowtail sashimi (see page 113)

Flying fish, salmon or sea urchin roe

Omelette

Cucumber

Avocado

Smoked salmon (or any smoked fish)

Instead of using wasabi, try Japanese mayonnaise or creamed cheese.

Note: As an unusual variation or in case you run out of nori sheets, *temaki* sushi may even be rolled in lettuce, particularly cos (comaine) or iceberg. Lettuce makes a light, refreshing roll.

Making Temaki Sushi

1. Start by picking up a sheet of nori in 1 hand and a handful of rice about the size of a golf ball in the other.

2. Place rice on one side of nori sheet and start spreading it out, remembering to cover only half of nori sheet.

3. With your finger or a spoon, rub the desired amount of wasabi along rice.

4. Add desired fillings to roll, placing them from one corner down to the middle of the opposite side.

5. Fold the nearest corner of nori over the filling, and start to shape into a cone.

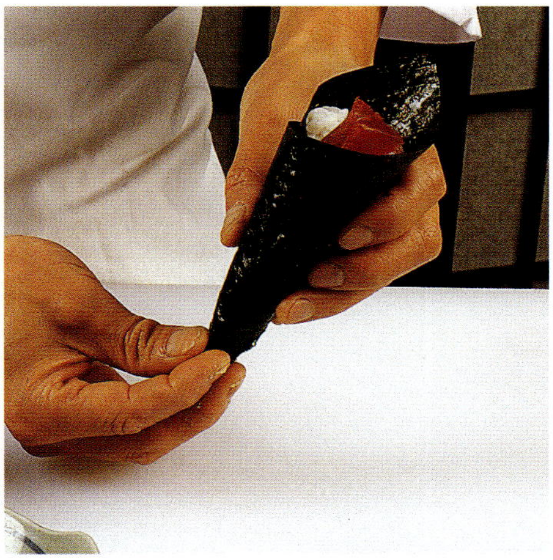

6. The finished *temaki* sushi should be coned-shaped with no rice falling out of the bottom.

Sashimi Cuts

There are 5 basic fish-cutting methods for sashimi and sushi. A very sharp, heavy knife is indispensable for them all.

Thread cut (Ito zukeri)

Although this technique may be used with any small fish, it is especially suitable for squid. Cut the squid straight down into $^1/_2$cm/$^1/_4$in slices, then cut lengthways into $^1/_2$cm/$^1/_4$in wide strips.

Cubic cut (Kazu giri)

This style of cutting is more often used for tuna. Cut the tuna as for the flat cut , then cut into 1cm/$^1/_2$in cubes.

Paper-thin cut (Usu zukuri)

Place any white fish fillet, such as bream or snapper, on a flat surface and, holding quite firmly with one hand, slice it at an angle into almost transparent sheets.

Flat cut (Hira giri):

This is the most popular shape, suitable for any filleted fish. Holding the fish firmly, cut straight down in slices about $^{1}/_{2}$-1cm/ $^{1}/_{4}$ - $^{1}/_{2}$in and 5cm/2in wide, depending on the size of the fillet.

Angled cut (sorigiri):

This is the ideal cut for sushi topping. Starting with a rectangular piece of fish, such as tuna, cut a trianglar piece from one corner, and continue slicing off pieces approximately $^{1}/_{2}$ - 1cm/$^{1}/_{4}$ - $^{1}/_{2}$in thick.

Tuna Sashimi (Maguru)

Ingredients

300g/10$^{1}/_{2}$ oz sashimi-grade tuna fillet

TOSA JUYA (DIPPING SAUCE):

3 tablespoons soy sauce

2$^{1}/_{2}$ teaspoons sake

5 teaspoons dried bonito (*katsuobushi*)

Method

1. Proceed to cut tuna into flat-cuts as described on page 109.

2. To make dipping sauce, put soy sauce, sake and dried bonito into a small saucepan and bring to the boil, stirring constantly, for 2 minutes.

3. Strain through a fine sieve and cool to room temperature. Divide dipping sauce among small dishes, and serve with tuna sashimi.

Note: If the fillet you have purchased has already been cut into a 'block', you can proceed to cut fish into the sashimi. On the other hand, if the fillet has not been trimmed and shaped into a block, then you may need to buy a larger fillet and trim it down to size yourself, perhaps using the off-cuts as minced tuna.

Salmon Sashimi (Sake)

Ingredients

300g/10½ oz sashimi-grade salmon or 1 whole salmon

shredded daikon radish

Method

1. If purchasing a whole salmon, proceed to clean, gut and fillet the fish as described on pages 5–6.

2. Trim away any dark or bruised flesh that may be evident, as well as any skin and 'fatty' flesh.

3. Shape fillets into a block, and apply the flat-cut, cutting off required number of pieces. Refer to page 109 for how to do the flat cut.

4. Arrange on a plate and garnish with shredded daikon radish.

Bonito Sashimi (Katsuo)

Ingredients

1 whole bonito (2kg/4½ lb)

1 teaspoon ginger, grated

Method

1. Clean, gut and fillet the bonito as described on pages 5–6.

2. Straight cut the fillets, (leaveing skin on).

3. Arrange on a serving plate, and garnish with grated ginger.

Note: Bonito is a widely distributed fish, with varieties found around the world. The flesh is pink-red in colour with a coarse grain and a rich flavour. If purchasing in fillet form, look for firm, moist flesh and marbling.

Colour is a good indicator of the freshness of fish. A freshly cut surface is very dull.

Pickled Whiting Sashimi (kisu)

Ingredients

2 fresh whole whiting (300g/10oz ea)

2 tablespoons salt

1 cup rice vinegar

Method

1. Clean, gut and fillet whiting as described on page 5–6.

2. Sprinkle salt all over fillets and allow to stand for 10–15 minutes. Then rinse in clean water.

3. Place fillets in a bowl and cover with rice vinegar. Allow to stand for a further 10 minutes.

5. Remove fillets from vinegar and drain in a colander.

6. Cut fillets into squares or using paper-thin cut, as described on pages 108–109.

Lobster Sashimi (Ise Ebi)

Ingredients

1 whole green (uncooked) lobster

shredded daikon radish

Method

1. If lobster is purchased frozen, allow to defrost overnight in the refrigerator Then, remove the head and reserve for garnish.

2. Use poultry scissors to make a clean cut in the tail shell. Pull lobster meat out, and stuff the empty shell with shredded daikon radish for presentation. Cut lobster meat into small sashimi slices.

3. Lay meat on the daikon bedded tail, and serve.

Note: Traditionally, lobsters that were to be prepared as sashimi were purchased live and killed moments before being presented and served. The Japanese obsession with absolute freshness made this practise commonplace.

Scampi Sashimi (Tenagaebi)

Ingredients

8 freshscampi (if unavailable use frozen)

***CHIRIZU* (SPICY DIPPING SAUCE):**

5 teaspoons sake

3 tablespoons freshly grated daikon radish

2 spring onions, finely sliced

3 tablespoons soy sauce

3 tablespoons lemon juice

$^1/_8$ teaspoon *hichimi togarashi* (seven-pepper spice)

Instructions

1. To prepare scampi, remove heads and set aside for garnish.

2. Peel back the under-side shell from the top down to the tail. Remove the flesh and discard the shells except for the bottom part of tail.

3. Place scampi meat on plate, putting head and tail on as garnish.

4. To make the dipping sauce, warm sake in a small saucepan, then ignite it with a match, off the heat. Shake the pan gently until the flame dies out. Allow to cool.

5. Put sake with the other ingredients and mix well. Pour into individual bowls and serve with scampi. This dipping sauce goes well with any other sashimi.

Note: The scampi, or deep sea lobster as it is also called, is targeted by trawlers mostly off north-western Australia. They are generally snap-frozen on-board the trawlers, thus making the job of finding fresh specimens a lot more difficult. Scampi has a wonderfully sweet flesh, ideal for sashimi.

Cuttlefish Sashimi (Ika)

Ingredients

6 cuttlefish (or squid)

3 nori sheets

1 cucumber, cut into slices 10cm/4in long

1 teaspoon flying fish roe

METHOD

1. Clean cuttlefish in the same way as squid, as described on page 10.

2. To make cuttlefish and cucumber rolls, cut cuttlefish and nori into a sheet 5x10cm/2x4in. Score the cuttlefish at 1/2 cm/ 1/4in intervals. Place scored cuttlefish face down, lie nori on top, then cucumber and flying fish roe. Roll up and cut into 1cm/1/2in slices.

6. To make cuttlefish and nori rolls, cut nori and cuttlefish into same size and place nori on top of cuttlefish. Lightly score through nori and into the cuttlefish and proceed to roll and cut into 1cm/1/2in slices. Cuttlefish can also be cut into the thread-shape cut, as described on page 108–109. Garnish with shredded nori.

Note: Cuttlefish is a mollusc and is generally smaller than a squid. It is highly prized in Japanese cuisine, with a flavour superior to that of the squid.
When buying cuttlefish, look for firm flesh and undamaged bodies. Don't be put off by a broken ink sac; they are often broken when they are caught. Clean in the same manner as you would a squid.

outdoor cooking

Swordfish and Pineapple Kebabs

Ingredients

12 bamboo skewers, soaked in water for 30 minutes

750g/1¾ lb swordfish steaks, cut into large cubes

½ fresh pineapple, cut into cubes same size as fish

1 green capsicum (bell pepper), cut into pieces same size as fish

FRESH MINT MARINADE:

3 tablespoons chopped fresh mint

2 teaspoons mint relish

½ cup white wine

juice of ½ lime or lemon

2 tablespoons red wine vinegar

1 teaspoon olive oil

freshly ground black pepper

Method

1. Thread swordfish, pineapple and green pepper, alternately onto skewers. Place prepared skewers in a shallow glass or ceramic dish.

2. To make marinade: Place mint, mint relish, wine, lime or lemon juice, vinegar, oil and black pepper to taste in a screwtop jar. Shake to combine. Pour over skewers. Cover and marinate in the refrigerator for 15 minutes.

3. Preheat the barbecue or grill until hot. Lightly spray or brush with unsaturated oil. Cook kebabs on the barbecue or under grill for 3–5 minutes each side or until fish just starts to flake when tested with a fork.

Makes 12 kebabs

Thai Prawn Cakes

Ingredients

500g/1 lb uncooked prawns, deveined

1/4 cup/30g/1oz chopped green onions

1 teaspoon ground lemon grass

2 kaffir lime or lemon myrtle leaves, soaked in boiling water for 15 minutes, finely chopped, optional

1 egg white

1 tablespoon Thai fish sauce (*nam pla*)

1 tablespoon fresh lime juice

1 teaspoon sweet chilli sauce or to taste

1/2 cup breadcrumbs, made from stale bread

2 tablespoons chopped fresh mint

2 tablespoons chopped fresh coriander

CORIANDER DIPPING SAUCE:

2 tablespoons chopped fresh coriander (cilantro)

1 green onion, finely chopped

1 clove garlic, crushed

1 teaspoon brown or palm sugar

1/2 cup rice or sherry vinegar

2 teaspoons reduced-salt soy sauce

1/2 teaspoon chilli sauce, optional

Method

1. Place prawns in a food processor. Using the pulse button, process to chop roughly. Add green onions, ground lemon grass, lime or lemon myrtle leaves, egg white, fish sauce, lime juice and chilli sauce. Using the pulse button, process until just combined. Transfer prawnmixture to a bowl. Fold in breadcrumbs, mint and coriander.

2. Shape prawn mixture into 5cm/2in round cakes. Place on a plate lined with plastic food wrap, or thread 2–3 patties on a lemon grass skewer. Cover. Refrigerate for 30 minutes or until cakes are firm.

3. Preheat the barbecue to a medium heat. Add cakes and cook for 2–3 minutes each side or until lightly browned. Alternatively, heat a nonstick frying pan over a medium heat, and lightly spray or brush with unsaturated oil and panfry. Or cook under a medium grill or bake in the oven at 210°C/410°F. If baking do not thread onto lemon grass skewers.

4. To make sauce, place coriander (cilantro), green onion, garlic, sugar, vinegar and soy and chilli sauces in a bowl. Whisk to combine. Serve with prawn cakes for dipping.

Serves 4 as a main meal or 8 as a starter

Barbecued Marinated Prawns

Ingredients

1kg/2¼ lb uncooked medium prawns, shelled and deveined, tails left on

CHILLI AND HERB MARINADE:

2 fresh red chillies, chopped

2 cloves garlic, crushed

1 tablespoon chopped fresh oregano

1 tablespoon chopped fresh parsley

½ cup olive oil

2 tablespoons balsamic vinegar

freshly ground black pepper

Method

1. Preheat the barbecue to a medium heat.

2. To make marinade, place chillies, garlic, oregano, parsley, oil, vinegar and black pepper to taste in a bowl and mix to combine. Add prawns, toss to coat and marinate for 10 minutes.

3. Drain prawns, and cook on the lightly oiled barbecue for 1–2 minutes each side or until prawns just change colour.

Serves 8

Hot Chilli Prawns

Ingredients

1½ kg/3⅓ lb uncooked large prawns, peeled and deveined , tails left on

CHILLI MARINADE:

2 teaspoons cracked black pepper

2 tablespoons sweet chilli sauce

1 tablespoon soy sauce

1 clove garlic, crushed

¼ cup lemon juice

MANGO CREAM:

1 mango, peeled, stoned and roughly chopped

3 tablespoons coconut milk

Method

1. To make marinade, place black pepper, chilli sauce, soy sauce, garlic and lemon juice in a bowl and mix to combine. Add prawns, toss to coat, cover and set aside to marinate for 1 hour. Toss several times during marinating.

2. To make mango cream, place mango flesh and coconut milk in a food processor or blender, and process until smooth.

3. Preheat the barbecue to a medium heat. Drain prawns and cook on the lightly oiled barbecue for 3–4 minutes or until prawns change colour. Serve immediately with mango cream.

Note: Coconut milk can be purchased in a number of forms: canned, as a long-life product in cartons, or as a powder to which you add water. Once opened it should be used within a day or so. It is available from Asian food stores and some supermarkets. If you have trouble finding it you can easily make your own. To make coconut milk, place 500g/1 lb desiccated coconut in a bowl and add 3 cups of boiling water. Set aside to stand for 30 minutes, then strain, squeezing the coconut to extract as much liquid as possible. This will make a thick coconut milk. The coconut can be used again to make a weaker coconut milk.

Serves 6

Prawn Satays

Ingredients

1kg/2$^{1}/_{4}$ lb uncooked large prawns, shelled and deveined, tails left intact

8 bamboo skewers, soaked in water for 30 minutes

SATAY SAUCE:

2 teaspoons vegetable oil

1 onion, chopped

3 teaspoons ground cumin

1 cup crunchy peanut butter

1 cup chicken stock

3 tablespoons soy sauce

Method

1. Thread prawns onto 8 skewers.

2. To make sauce, heat oil in a saucepan, add onion and cumin and cook, stirring, for 3 minutes or until onion is soft. Add peanut butter, stock and soy sauce, and cook over a medium heat, stirring, for 5 minutes or until sauce boils and thickens.

3. Brush prawns with sauce and cook on a preheated barbecue grill for 2 minutes each side or until prawns change colour. To serve, drizzle with any remaining sauce.

Makes 8 satays

Seafood Paella

(opposite)

Ingredients

1 tablespoon olive oil

2 onions, chopped

2 cloves garlic, crushed

1 tablespoon fresh thyme leaves

2 teaspoons finely grated lemon rind

4 ripe tomatoes, chopped

2$^{1}/_{2}$ cups short grain white rice
pinch saffron threads soaked in 2 cups water

5 cups chicken or fish stock

300g/10$^{1}/_{2}$ oz fresh or frozen peas

2 red capsicums (peppers), chopped

1kg/2$^{1}/_{4}$ lb mussels, scrubbed and beards removed

500g/1 lb firm white fish fillets, chopped

315g/11oz peeled uncooked prawns

225g/8oz scallops

3 squid tubes, sliced

1 tablespoon chopped fresh parsley

Method

1. Preheat the barbecue to a medium heat. Place a large paella or frying pan on to the barbecue, add oil and heat. Add onions, garlic, thyme and lemon rind and cook for 3 minutes or until onion is soft.

2. Add tomatoes and cook, stirring, for 4 minutes. Add rice and cook, stirring, for 4 minutes longer or until rice is translucent. Stir in saffron mixture and stock and bring to simmering point. Simmer, stirring occasionally, for 30 minutes or until rice has absorbed almost all of the liquid.

3. Stir in peas, red capsicum (pepper) and mussels, and cook for 2 minutes. Add fish, prawns and scallops and cook, stirring, for 2–3 minutes. Stir in squid and parsley and cook, stirring, for 1–2 minutes or until seafood is cooked.

Serves 8

Cod with Basil Aïoli

Ingredients

1 clove garlic, minced

2 tablespoons olive oil

1 tablespoon lemon juice

4 cod cutlets

BASIL AIOLI:

1 cup basil leaves

$^1/_2$ cup olive oil

1 clove garlic, minced

2 egg yolks

3 teaspoons lemon juice

1 tablespoon water

freshly ground black pepper

salt, to taste

Method

1. Combine garlic, olive oil and lemon juice in a dish, and marinate fish cutlets, for 1 hour.

2. In a food processor, place basil, 1 tablespoon oil, garlic, egg yolks and lemon juice. Process until well combined. With the processor running, add oil in a thin stream and process until thick. Add water to make a thinner aïoli.

3. Grease a chargrill plate or frying pan, and grill fish for 3 minutes, on each side.

4. Serve immediately with basil aïoli

Serves 4

Sardines with Roasted Capsicum

Ingredients

1 - 2 tablespoons olive oil

255g/9oz sardine fillets (16 sardines)

1 tablespoon lemon juice

2 red capsicums (peppers), roasted and thinly sliced

200g/7oz baby spinach or rocket, washed and trimmed

DRESSING:

55mL/2fl oz virgin olive oil, extra

45mL/1½ fl oz lemon juice, extra

1 tablespoon oregano, chopped

freshly ground pepper and salt

2 red capsicums (bell peppers), roasted and thinly sliced

200g/7oz baby spinach or rocket, washed and trimmed

Method

1. Lightly brush a chargrill pan with oil, and heat. Lightly brush sardines with oil, then add to pan and cook for 1–2 minutes on each side. Set aside on a plate, and pour lemon juice over sardines.

2. Combine the olive oil, extra lemon juice, oregano, pepper and salt. Mix until well combined.

2. On individual serving plates add spinach or rocket, slices of red capsicum (pepper), 4 sardines on top and drizzle with dressing. Serve immediately.

Serves 4

Swordfish Kebabs with Tomato Sauce

Ingredients

1 tablespoon olive oil

1 small onion, finely diced

2 cloves garlic, crushed

2 x 400g/14oz cans tomatoes, drained

1/2 teaspoon sugar

1/2 teaspoon salt

freshly ground black pepper

1/2 cup fresh basil, torn

750g/1 2/3 lb swordfish

1 green capsicum (pepper), deseeded

1 medium eggplant (aubergine)

8 bamboo skewers, soaked in water for 30 minutes

6 sprigs rosemary

40mL/1 1/3 fl oz olive oil

1 tablespoon rosemary, chopped

salt and freshly ground black pepper

1 lemon, cut into 4 wedges

Method

1. To make the sauce, heat the oil in a large saucepan, and sauté the onion and garlic over a low heat until transparent. Add tomatoes, sugar, salt and pepper. Simmer gently for 20 minutes. Add basil, and keep warm.

2. Pre-heat barbecue to moderate heat.

3. Cut swordfish, green capsicum (pepper) and eggplant (aubergine) into large cubes. Arrange on 8 bamboo skewers alternating with the rosemary sprigs. Brush with olive oil, sprinkle with chopped rosemary and season with salt and pepper.

6. Grill kebabs, turning over at least once to brown the sides. Baste with a little sauce. The swordfish should be golden, with herbs and vegetables slightly charred.

7. Serve with extra tomato sauce and lemon wedges.

Serves 4

Oysters and Mussels in Shells

Ingredients

500g/1 lb mussels, scrubbed and beards removed

24 oysters in half shells

55g/2oz butter, softened

1 tablespoon chopped fresh parsley

2 tablespoons lemon juice

1 tablespoon orange juice

1 tablespoon white wine

Method

1. Preheat the barbecue to a high heat. Place mussels and oysters on barbecue grill, and cook for 3–5 minutes or until mussel shells open and oysters are warm. Discard any mussels that do not open after 5 minutes of cooking.

2. Place butter, parsley, lemon juice, orange juice and wine in a heavy-based saucepan, place on the barbecue and cook, stirring, for 2 minutes or until mixture is bubbling. Place mussels and oysters on a serving platter, drizzle with butter mixture and serve immediately.

Note: Mussels will live out of water for up to 7 days if treated correctly. To keep mussels alive, place them in a bucket, cover with a wet towel and top with ice. Store in a cool place, and as the ice melts, drain off the water and replace ice. It is important that the mussels do not sit in the water or they will drown.

Serves 6

Salmon Cutlets with Pineapple Salsa

Ingredients

4 salmon cutlets, cut 2½ cm/1in thick

PINEAPPLE SALSA:

255g/9oz roughly chopped fresh or canned pineapple

2 spring onions, finely chopped

1 fresh red chilli, seeded and finely chopped

1 tablespoon lemon juice

2 tablespoons finely chopped fresh mint

1 lemon, cut into 4 wedges

Method

1. Preheat the barbecue to a medium heat. Cook salmon cutlets on the lightly oiled barbecue for 3–5 minutes each side or until flesh flakes when tested with a fork.

2. To make salsa, place pineapple, spring onions, chilli, lemon juice and mint in a food processor or blender and process to combine. Serve at room temperature with salmon cutlets, lemon wedges and steamed asparagus spears.

Note: This salsa is delicious served with any fish or barbecued chicken.

Serves 4

Home-Smoked Trout

Ingredients

1 cup smoking chips

$^1/_2$ cup white wine

4 small rainbow trout, cleaned, with head and tail intact

1 tablespoon vegetable oil

3 red onions, thinly sliced

1 lemon, thinly sliced

8 sprigs dill

Method

1. Place smoking chips and wine in a non-reactive metal dish and stand for 1 hour.

2. Preheat the covered barbecue to a low heat. Place dish, with smoking chips in, in the barbecue over hot coals, and cover barbecue with lid.Heat for 5–10 minutes or until wine is hot.

3. Place trout on a wire rack set in a roasting tin. Brush trout lightly with oil, then top with onions, lemon and dill. Position roasting tin containing trout on rack in the barbecue, cover barbecue with lid and smoke for 15–20 minutes or until trout flakes when tested with fork.

Note: This recipe is also suitable for a smoke-box.

Serves 4

Salmon Skewers

Ingredients

500g/1 lb salmon fillet, cut into $2^1/_2$ cm/1in squares

255g/9oz snow peas (*mangetout*), trimmed

1 tablespoon wholegrain mustard

2 teaspoons chopped fresh lemon thyme or thyme

$^1/_2$ teaspoon ground cumin

2 tablespoons lemon juice

2 teaspoons honey

Method

1. Preheat the barbecue to a medium heat. Thread salmon and snow peas (*mangetout*), alternately, onto lightly oiled skewers.

2. Place mustard, thyme, cumin, lemon juice and honey in a bowl and mix to combine. Brush mustard mixture over salmon, and cook on the lightly oiled barbecue grill for 2–3 minutes on each side or until salmon is just cooked.

Serves 4

Blackened Tuna Steaks

Ingredients

4 thick tuna steaks

2 tablespoons olive oil

lemons for serving

CAJUN SEASONING:

2 tablespoons sweet paprika

1 tablespoon dried ground garlic

1 tablespoon onion powder

2 teaspoons crushed black peppercorns

2 teaspoons dried mixed herbs

1 teaspoon cayenne pepper

FENNEL TOMATO SALSA:

4 plum (egg or Italian) tomatoes, chopped

1 bulb fennel, finely chopped

1 red onion, finely chopped

2 tablespoons capers

1 tablespoon chopped fresh mint

1 clove garlic, crushed

1 tablespoon lemon juice

1 tablespoon orange juice

Method

1. Preheat the barbecue to a high heat. To make salsa, place tomatoes, fennel, onion, capers, mint, garlic, lemon juice and orange juice in a bowl and toss to combine. Set aside until ready to serve.

2. To make Cajun seasoning, place paprika, ground garlic, onion powder, black peppercorns, herbs and cayenne pepper in a bowl and mix to combine. Add tuna, toss to coat and shake off excess.

3. Heat oil on the barbecue plate for 2–3 minutes or until hot. Add tuna and cook for 3–4 minutes on each side or until blackened and cooked to your liking. Serve immediately with salsa and lemon.

Note: If tuna is unavailable swordfish or salmon are delicious alternatives. Dried ground garlic is available in the spice section of supermarkets. It has a pungent taste and aroma and should be used with care.

Serves 4

Sesame Barbecued Prawns

Ingredients

1kg/2 1/4 lb medium-large king prawns

55mL/2fl oz olive oil

55mL/2fl oz red wine

4 shallots, finely chopped

1 teaspoon grated lemon rind

1/2 teaspoon cracked black pepper

12 bamboo skewers, soaked in water for 30 minutes

115g/4oz toasted sesame seeds

Method

1. Peel and devein prawns, leaving the shell tails intact.

2. Combine oil, wine, shallots, lemon rind and pepper and mix well.

3. Thread prawns onto bamboo skewers (approximately 3 per skewer). Place skewers in a shallow dish, and pour marinade over. Allow to marinate for at least 1 hour.

4. Roll prawns in toasted sesame seeds, pressing them on well. Refrigerate for 30 minutes before cooking.

6. Cook on the hot plate of a well-heated barbecue for 2 minutes each side. Brush with marinade during cooking.

Serves 6-8

Vietnamese Barbecued Prawns

Ingredients

500g/1 lb large green prawns

200g/7oz thin rice vermicelli

2 teaspoons vegetable oil

6 green shallots, chopped

½ cup roasted peanuts

½ bunch coriander (cilantro) leaves, chopped

***NUOC CHAM* SAUCE:**

2 garlic cloves, peeled

2 dried red chillies

5 teaspoons sugar

juice and pulp of 1½ limes

4 tablespoons Thai fish sauce (nam pla)

5 tablespoons water

Method

1. To make sauce, pound garlic, chillies and sugar using a pestle and mortar. Add lime juice and pulp, then fish sauce and water. Mix well to combine.

2. Slit prawns down back, remove vein, wash and pat dry. Cook prawns over charcoal for about 5 minutes, turning once.

3. Add rice vermicelli to boiling water, and boil for 2 minutes. Drain and rinse under cold, running water.

4. Heat oil in a wok or frying pan, and add green shallots and fry until softened. Arrange rice vermicelle on warmed serving plates, top with prawns, then sprinkle with shallots and peanuts. Pour sauce over the top and sprinkle with chopped coriander (cilantro).

Serves 4

Coriander Swordfish Steaks

Ingredients

115g/4oz unsalted butter

2 tablespoons finely chopped coriander (cilantro)

1 tablespoon grated Parmesan cheese

4 swordfish steaks

1 tablespoon olive oil

4 zucchinis (courgettes), cut into long slices

1 red capsicum (pepper), quartered

Method

1. Cream butter until soft and mix in coriander and parmesan. Pile into a butter pot and set aside.

2. Preheat barbecue grill until hot and brush with oil. Brush fish steaks with oil, place on grill bars and cook for 3–4 minutes on each side according to thickness. Brush or spray vegetables with extra oil and place on grill for a few minutes on each side.

3. Remove fish steaks and vegetables from the grill to heated plates. Top each swordfish steak with a generous dollop of coriander butter mixture and serve immediately.

Serves 4

Scallops and Prawns en Brochette

Ingredients

225g/8oz pickling onions

6 bacon rashers

500g/1 lb green prawns, peeled and deveived, with tails intact

400g/14oz scallops

12 bamboo skewers, soaked in water for 30 minutes

2 tablespoons olive oil

55g/2oz butter

2 tablespoons fresh dill, chopped

2 tablespoons parsely, chopped

2 spring onions, finely chopped

2 cloves garlic, crushed

freshly ground black pepper

2 tablespoons lemon juice

2 teaspoons grated lemon rind

Method

1. Parboil onions until almost tender, then drain and rinse under cold water. Remove rind from bacon and cut each rasher into 3, then roll each section up.

2. Thread prawns, scallops and bacon onto bamboo skewers, finishing with an onion on the end of each one.

3. Combine oil, butter, dill, parsley, spring onions, garlic, pepper, lemon juice and rind in a dish. Add seafood skewers and stand for at least 1 hour.

4. Remove seafood skewers from marinade and cook on a preheated barbecue grill until tender, brushing occasionally with marinade.

Serves 6

Skewered Prawns

Ingredients

500g/1 lb green prawns

MARINADE:

1 small onion, finely chopped

2 cloves garlic, crushed

1 teaspoon fresh ginger, chopped

55mL/2fl oz dry sherry

55mL/2fl oz olive oil

salt and freshly ground black pepper

12 bamboo skewers, soaked in water for 30 minutes

Method

1. Wash prawns thoroughly. Do not remove shells.

2. Mix together all ingredients to make marinade. Pour over prawns, and let stand for 1–2 hours in the refrigerator.

3. Thread prawns onto skewers. Grill or barbecue for about 10 minutes, turning several times. Serve immediately.

Serves 4

Barbecued Chilli Prawns (opposite)

Ingredients

1 kg/2¼ lb medium-sized uncooked prawns, in their shells

255g/9oz chopped pawpaw

2 tablespoons chopped fresh mint

lime wedges

sliced chillies

ORANGE MARINADE:

2 tablespoons mild chilli powder

2 tablespoons chopped fresh oregano

2 cloves garlic, crushed

2 teaspoons grated orange rind

2 teaspoons grated lime rind

¼ cup orange juice

¼ cup lime juice

Method

1. To make marinade, place chilli powder, oregano, garlic, orange and lime rinds and orange and lime juices in a bowl and mix to combine. Add prawns, toss, cover and marinate in the refrigerator for 1 hour.

2. Drain prawns and cook on a preheated hot chargrill or barbecue plate for 1 minute on each side or until they change colour.

3. Place pawpaw and mint in a bowl and toss to combine. To serve, pile prawns onto serving plates, top with pawpaw mixture and accompany with lime wedges and sliced chillies.

Serves 4

Honey and Chilli Prawns

Ingredients

500g/1 lb green king prawns

$^1/_4$ cup red wine

$^1/_2$ cup honey

$^1/_4$ teaspoon ground chilli

1 teaspoon mustard powder

bamboo skewers, soaked in water for 30 minutes

Method

1. Mix all ingredients except prawns together to make marinade.

2. Shell prawns, devain and leave on tails. Place in a glass dish and add enough marinade to coat well. Cover and marinate in the refrigerator for 1 hour. Thread prawns onto the bamboo skewers, either through the side or through the length.

3. Preheat the barbecue to medium-high. Place a sheet of baking paper over the grill bars and place prawns on the paper. Cook for 4–5 minutes each side: they will turn pink when cooked. Brush with marinade while cooking. Transfer to a platter and serve immediately.

Serves 3-4

Teriyaki Prawns

Ingredients

1kg/2¼ lb fresh green prawns in their shells

bamboo skewers, soaked in water for 30 minutes

TERIYAKI MARINADE:

½ cup soy sauce

2 tablespoons brown sugar

½ teaspoon ground ginger

2 tablespoons wine vinegar

1 clove garlic, crushed

2 tablespoons tomato sauce

Method

1. To make marinade, mix all ingredients together and let stand for 1 hour for flavours to mix.

2. Shell prawns, leaving tails intact. Place in a non-metal dish and smother with the marinade. Cover and refrigerate for 1–2 hours. Thread onto soaked skewers. For small prawns thread 2–3 per skewer; for king prawns thread only 1 from tail-end to top.

3. Heat the barbecue and place a square of baking paper on the grill bars. Place prawns on the grill, brushing with marinade on both sides as they cook. Cook until prawns turn pink in colour. Take care not to overcook.

Serves 4

Skewers with Tomato Sauce

Ingredients

750g/1⅔ lb white fish, cubed

6 skewers, lightly oiled

¼ cup lime juice

freshly ground black pepper

6 corn or flour tortillas, warmed

2 tablespoons chopped fresh coriander (cilantro)

lime wedges

TOMATO, OLIVE AND CAPER SAUCE:

1 tablespoon olive oil

1 onion, finely chopped

1 clove garlic, crushed

4 ripe tomatoes, chopped

85g/3 oz green olives

2 jalapeño chillies, chopped

2 tablespoons capers, drained

2 tablespoons chopped fresh flat-leaf parsley

black pepper to taste

Method

1. Thread fish onto 6 lightly oiled skewers, brush with lime juice and season with black pepper to taste. Set aside.

2. To make sauce, heat oil in a frying pan over a medium heat, add onion and garlic and cook, stirring, for 2 minutes or until onion is soft. Add tomatoes, olives, chillies, capers and parsley, and cook, stirring, for 5 minutes or until sauce is warm. Season with black pepper to taste.

3. Cook fish skewers on a preheated hot barbecue or chargrill for 1 minute on each side or until tender. To serve, place fish skewers on tortillas, spoon over sauce, scatter with coriander and accompany with lime wedges.

Serves 6

Garlic Lobster Tails with Exotic Salad

Ingredients

6 green (raw) lobster tails

85g/3oz butter, softened

2 teaspoons crushed garlic

2 tablespoons honey and lemon marinade

EXOTIC SALAD

1 avocado, cut into $^1/_2$cm/$^1/_4$ in dice

2 Lebanese cucumbers, diced

$^1/_2$ small rockmelon, peeled and diced

$^1/_3$ cup honey and lemon marinade

HONEY and LEMON MARINADE:

$^1/_2$ cup olive oil

2 tablespoons lemon juice

1 tablespoon honey

1 tablespoon freshly crushed garlic

2 bay leaves, crushed

Method

1. To make marinade, combine all ingredients in a bowl and mix well.

2. With kitchen scissors, cut each side of the soft shell on the underside of lobster tails, and remove. Run a metal skewer through the length of each tail to keep them flat while cooking. Soften butter and mix in garlic, and honey and lemon marinade. Spread over lobster meat, reserving a little butter mixture.

3. Prepare salad before cooking lobster tails. Mix avocado, cucumber and rockmelon together. Pour honey and lemon marinade over the salad. Refrigerate until required.

4. Heat the barbecue to medium-high and oil the grill bars. Place lobster tails shell-side down and cook until shell turns red. Spread mixture with more butter and turn meat-side down and cook for 5–8 minutes or until meat turns white. Turn again and cook 2 minutes more shell-side down. Remove skewers and place on warm plates. Dot with any remaining butter mixture, and serve immediately with salad.

Serves 4-6

Bacon and Prawns

Ingredients

1 tablespoon Dijon mustard

1 clove garlic, crushed

$^1/_2$ red capsicum (pepper), finely chopped

1 tablespoon finely chopped fresh dill

2 tablespoons olive oil

2 tablespoons lemon juice

freshly ground black pepper

12 large cooked prawns, shelled with tails left intact

4 rashers lean bacon, cut into 12 $7^1/_2$ cm/3 in strips

Method

1. Place mustard, garlic, red capsicum (pepper), dill, oil, lemon juice and black pepper to taste in a bowl and mix to combine. Add prawns and toss to coat. Set aside to marinate for 30 minutes.

2. Preheat the barbecue to a high heat. Drain prawns and reserve marinade. Wrap a strip of bacon around each prawn and thread onto bamboo skewers. Brush with reserved marinade and cook onto lightly oiled barbecue, turning several times, for 2–3 minutes or until bacon is cooked and crisp.

Makes 4 kebabs

Avocado and Prawn Skewers

Ingredients

2 avocados, cut into cubes

3 tablespoons lemon juice

20 cooked large prawns, shelled

10 cherry tomatoes, halved

10 bamboo skewers, lightly oiled

TOMATO DIPPING SAUCE:

$^1/_2$ cup sour cream

$^1/_2$ cup mayonnaise

2 tablespoons tomato sauce

2 teaspoons Worcestershire sauce

Method

1. Place avocado cubes in a bowl, pour lemon juice over and toss to coat. Thread 2 prawns, 2 avocado cubes and 2 tomato halves, alternately, onto bamboo skewers.

2. To make dipping sauce, place sour cream, mayonnaise, tomato sauce and Worcestershire sauce in a bowl and mix to combine. Serve sauce with kebabs for dipping.

Makes 10 kebabs

exotic flavours

Sesame Coconut King Prawns with Mango Salsa

Ingredients

12 raw king prawns, peeled and tail left on

salt and pepper to taste

flour for dusting

1 egg, beaten

1 cup sesame seeds

1 cup coconut threads

MANGO SALSA:

1 mango, peeled and finely diced

$^{1}/_{2}$ small red onion, finely diced

2 tablespoons coriander (cilantro), chopped

juice of 1 lime

salt and pepper to taste

2 tablespoons butter or olive oil

assorted greens of your choice

Method

1. Butterfly prawns then, dust with salt, pepper and flour. Dip in egg, allowing the excess to run off, then dredge in a mixture of sesame seeds and coconut. Set aside.

2. To make salsa, mix the mango, onion, coriander (cilantro) and lime juice in a bowl and season to taste.

3. Heat butter or olive oil in a frying pan, add the prawns and fry over a high heat for 1–2 minutes each side until golden.

4. To serve, arrange some leaves on each plate and top with 3 cooked prawns and a generous spoonful of mango salsa.

Serves 4

Shellfish with Lemon Grass

Ingredients

5 red or golden shallots, chopped

4 stalks fresh lemon grass, bruised and cut into 3cm/1 1/2 in pieces, or 2 teaspoons dried lemon grass, soaked in hot water until soft

3 cloves garlic, chopped

5cm/2in piece fresh ginger, shredded

3 fresh red chillies, seeded and chopped

8 kaffir lime leaves, torn into pieces

750g/1 2/3 lb mussels, scrubbed and beards removed

1/4 cup water

12 scallops on shells, cleaned

1 tablespoon lime juice

1 tablespoon Thai fish sauce (*nam pla*)

3 tablespoons fresh basil leaves

Method

1. Place shallots, lemon grass, garlic, ginger, chillies and lime leaves in a small bowl and mix to combine.

2. Place mussels in a wok and sprinkle over half the shallot mixture. Pour in water, cover and cook over a high heat for 5 minutes.

3. Add scallops, remaining shallot mixture, lime juice, fish sauce and basil and toss to combine. Cover and cook for 4–5 minutes or until mussels and scallops are cooked. Discard any mussels that do not open after 5 minutes. Serve immediately

Serves 4

Thai Fish Burgers

Ingredients

500g/1 lb white fish fillets, bones removed

2 – 3 tablespoons red curry paste

85g/3oz green beans, thinly sliced

4 kaffir lime leaves, finely shredded

8 Thai basil leaves, finely shredded

1 tablespoon soybean oil

4 wholegrain rolls, halved

85g/3oz watercress, washed

1 Lebanese cucumber, very thinly sliced

1 carrot, very thinly sliced

DRESSING:

1 tablespoon sweet chilli sauce

1 tablespoon lime juice

$^1/_2$ cup reduced fat natural yoghurt

Method

1. Place roughly chopped fish in a food processor, add curry paste and process until smooth. Transfer fish paste to a bowl and stir in beans, kaffir lime leaves and basil and mix well to combine. Shape the mixture into four round, slightly flattened burgers.

2. Heat the oil in a large non-stick frying pan, add the burgers and cook over a medium heat for 15 minutes, turning once, or until they are cooked through.

3. Toast rolls and put watercress, cucumber and carrot on each base. Top each roll with a fish burger.

4. To make dressing, put sweet chilli sauce, lime juice and yoghurt in a bowl and whisk gently to combine.

5. Spoon dressing over burgers and cover with toasted roll tops.

Serves 4

Laksa

Ingredients

45mL/1$\frac{1}{2}$ fl oz peanut oil or vegetable oil

1 onion, finely chopped

3 cloves garlic, chopped

1 tablespoon Laksa paste

1$\frac{3}{5}$ cups chicken stock

1 stalk lemon grass chopped

500g/1 lb mussels, cleaned

1 cup coconut cream

145g/5oz rice noodles

1 kaffir lime leaf, finely chopped

Method

1. In a large saucepan on medium heat, put oil, onions, garlic and Laksa paste and cook for 3–5 minutes.

2. Add chicken stock, lemon grass and mussels and cook until mussels start to open.

3. Add coconut cream, rice noodles and lime leaf. Cook for another 4 minutes when all mussels have opened. Discard any mussels that do not open.

Serves 4

Barbecued Squid Salad

Ingredients

1 tablespoon chilli oil

1 tablespoon finely grated lemon rind

2 teaspoons crushed black peppercorns

500g/1 lb small squid hoods, cleaned

30g/1oz fresh basil leaves

30g/1oz fresh mint leaves

30g/1oz fresh coriander (cilantro) leaves

LEMON AND CHILLI DRESSING:

1 fresh green chilli, chopped

2 tablespoons brown sugar

3 tablespoons lemon juice

2 tablespoons light soy sauce

Method

1. Place chilli oil, lemon rind and peppercorns in a shallow dish and mix to combine. Add squid and marinate for 30 minutes.

2. Line a serving platter with basil, mint and coriander (cilantro). Cover with plastic food wrap and refrigerate until ready to serve.

3. To make dressing, place chilli, sugar, lemon juice and soy sauce in a bowl and mix to combine.

4. Preheat the barbecue, chargrill pan or frying pan and cook squid for 30 seconds on each side or until tender. Take care not to overcook squid or it will become tough. Place squid on top of herbs and drizzle with dressing.

Serves 4

Steamed Fish Rolls with Tomato Vinaigrette

Ingredients

4 boneless, skinless white fish fillets

2 tablespoons grapeseed oil

2 cloves garlic, crushed

6 spring onions, chopped

1 cup fresh wholemeal breadcrumbs

small bunch fresh basil leaves, chopped

small bunch fresh flat-leaf parsley, chopped

1 teaspoon lemon zest

2 tablespoons lemon juice

1 cup tomato juice

2 tablespoons white wine vinegar

1 tablespoon brown sugar

Method

1. Cut fish fillets in half lengthwise, following the natural centre line.

2. Heat 1 tablespoon of oil in a large nonstick frying pan, add garlic and spring onions and cook over a medium heat for 3 minutes or until spring onions are soft. Put in a food processor with breadcrumbs, half basil, half parsley and lemon zest and juice. Process to combine.

3. Divide the stuffing into 8 equal portions and roll into oblong shapes. Put a piece on the end of each piece of fish and roll up to enclose the filling. Secure with a toothpick or piece of string. Cover and refrigerate for 30 minutes.

4. Finely chop remaining basil and parsley and put into a saucepan with tomato juice, vinegar and brown sugar. Cook over a low heat until warm.

5. Put fish rolls in a large bamboo steamer lined with baking paper. Cover and put over a wok of simmering water, making sure the base of the steamer does not touch the water. Steam for 10 minutes or until fish is tender and the stuffing heated through.

6. Serve fish rolls drizzled with tomato vinaigrette and a crisp green salad.

Serves 4

Prawn and Ginger Ravioli

Ingredients

600g/21oz green prawns, peeled and deveined

1 clove garlic, chopped

1 tablespoon grated fresh ginger

2 spring onions, finely sliced

200g/7oz wonton wrappers

fresh coriander (cilantro) sprigs

a little water

DRESSING:

1 small red chilli, finely sliced

2 tablespoons Thai fish sauce (*nam pla*)

2 teaspoons grated palm sugar

2 teaspoons lime juice

1 tablespoon peanut oil

Method

1. Finely chop prawns, and place with garlic, ginger and spring onions in a bowl. Mix to combine.

2. Put a heaped teaspoon of mixture in the centre of wonton wrapper, lightly brush the edges with water and top with another wrapper. Press the edges firmly together to seal. Repeat with the remaining filling and wrappers.

3. Cook ravioli in batches in a large saucepan of rapidly boiling water for 5 minutes. Drain well and transfer to serving plates.

4. To make dressing, put chilli, fish sauce, palm sugar, lime juice and peanut oil in a jug and whisk to combine.

5. Drizzle dressing over ravioli, and serve topped with sprigs of fresh coriander.

Serves 4

Vietnamese Crêpes

Ingredients

CRÊPES

250g/8¾ oz rice flour

1 teaspoon salt

1½ teaspoons sugar

1 cup canned coconut milk

1 cup water

⅓ teaspoon ground turmeric

200g/7oz shelled king prawns

200g/7oz bean shoots

100g/3⅓ oz pork fillet or chicken

peanut oil (for frying)

1 onion, sliced

DRESSING:

3 teaspoons fish sauce

5 teaspoons sugar

2 tablespoons water

1 tiny red chilli, minced

1 clove garlic, minced

Vietnamese mint leaves

iceberg lettuce leaves

Method

1. To make the crêpes, prepare the batter by mixing together the rice flour, salt, sugar, coconut milk, water and turmeric until smooth.

2. Wash and dry prawns and chop roughly. Wash bean shoots and set aside. Dice the pork or chicken.

3. Heat a large frying pan and pour in a little oil. Add pork, onion and prawns, and cook, stirring constantly until prawns change colour and pork is cooked through.

4. Pour enough batter over the mixture to cover, top with some bean shoots and cover with a lid. Cook for 2 minutes until crisp. Turn over and cook the other side until golden.

5. Make dressing by mixing all the ingredients together. To serve, place a Vietnamese mint leaf on a piece of the crêpe. Enclose in a lettuce leaf and drizzle some dressing over. Eat immediately.

Variation: To make a vegetarian crêpe, replace the pork and prawns with 1 medium carrot and half a medium-sized red capsicum (both julienned finely) and proceed as above.

Serves 6

Fish Baked in Corn Husks

Ingredients

16 – 24 dried corn husks

4 firm white fish fillets

3 tablespoons fresh coriander (cilantro) leaves

1 avocado, sliced

pickled jalapeño chillies

corn or flour tortillas, warmed

CHILLI LIME PASTE:

3 cloves garlic, chopped

2 mild fresh green chillies, chopped

2 tablespoons fresh oregano leaves

2 tablespoons mild chilli powder

2 teaspoons grated lime rind

1 teaspoon ground cumin

$^1/_4$ cup lime juice

Method

1. Place corn husks in a bowl, pour over warm water to cover and soak for 30 minutes.

2. To make chilli lime paste, place garlic, chillies, oregano, chilli powder, lime rind, cumin and lime juice in a food processor or blender and process until smooth.

3. Cut each fish fillet in half, then spread both sides with chilli lime paste.

4. Overlap 2–3 corn husks, place a piece of fish on top, then cover with more husks, fold to enclose fish and tie to secure. Place parcels on a baking tray and bake for 10 – 12 minutes or until flesh flakes when tested with a fork.

5. To serve, open fish parcels, scatter with coriander and accompany with avocado, chillies and tortillas.

Serves 4

Prawn and Pineapple Curry

Ingredients

500g/1 lb green king prawns, shelled and deveined

1 stalk lemon grass, roughly chopped

5 spring onions, peeled

3 cloves garlic, peeled

4 fresh red chillies, halved and seeded

1 teaspoon ground turmeric

3 tablespoons chopped coriander (cilantro)

6 tablespoons vegetable oil

$^1/_2$ teaspoon shrimp paste

1 can coconut milk

1 can sliced pineapple, drained and chopped

salt, to taste

Method

1. Using a blender or food processor grind lemongrass with spring onions, garlic, chillies, turmeric and coriander.

2. Heat oil in a wok and add the curry. Cook for a minute, then stir in shrimp paste with the thin part of coconut milk. When mixture is bubbling, stir in the prawns and remaining coconut milk.

3. Allow to heat for a few minutes then stir in pineapple pieces and continue to simmer for about 10 minutes. Serve with steamed rice.

Serves 4

Pad Thai Noodles

Ingredients

315g/11oz fresh or dried rice noodles

2 teaspoons vegetable oil

4 red or golden shallots, chopped

3 fresh red chillies, chopped

2 tablespoons shredded fresh ginger

255g/9oz chicken breast fillets, chopped

255g/9oz medium uncooked prawns, shelled and deveined

55g/2oz roasted peanuts, chopped

1 tablespoon sugar

4 tablespoons lime juice

3 tablespoons Thai fish sauce (*nam pla*)

2 tablespoons light soy sauce

115g/4oz tofu, chopped

55g/2oz bean sprouts

4 tablespoons coriander (cilantro) leaves

3 tablespoons fresh mint leaves

lime wedges to serve

Method

1. Place noodles in a bowl and pour over boiling water to cover. If using fresh noodles soak for 2 minutes; if using dried noodles soak for 5–6 minutes or until soft. Drain well and set aside.

2. Heat oil in a frying pan or wok over a high heat, add shallots, chillies and ginger, and stir-fry for 1 minute. Add chicken and prawns, and stir-fry for 4 minutes or until cooked.

3. Add noodles, peanuts, sugar, lime juice and fish and soy sauces and stir-fry for 4 minutes or until heated through. Stir in tofu, bean sprouts, coriander (cilantro) and mint, and cook for 1–2 minutes. Serve with lime wedges.

Serves 4

Chilli Tempura

Ingredients

vegetable oil for deep-frying

500g/1 lb uncooked large prawns, peeled, deveined and tails left intact

12 snow peas (*mangetout*), trimmed

1 eggplant (aubergine), cut into thin slices

1 small head broccoli, broken into small florets

TEMPURA BATTER:

3/4 cup self-raising flour

1/2 cup cornflour

1 teaspoon chilli powder

1 egg, lightly beaten

1 cup iced water

4 ice cubes

Method

1. To make batter, place flour, cornflour and chilli powder in a bowl, mix to combine and make a well in the centre. Whisk in egg and water and beat until smooth. Add ice cubes.

2. Heat oil in a deep saucepan until a cube of bread dropped in browns in 50 seconds.

3. Dip prawns, snow peas (*mangetout*), eggplant (aubergine) and broccoli florets in batter and deep-fry a few at a time for 3–4 minutes or until golden and crisp. Serve immediately.

Serving suggestion: All that is needed to make this a complete meal is a variety of purchased dipping sauces, chutneys, relishes and a tossed green salad.

Serves 4

Mussels with Coconut Vinegar

Ingredients

$1^1/_2$ kg/$3^1/_3$ lb mussels in their shells

6 whole coriander plants, washed and roughly chopped

3 stalks fresh lemon grass, bruised, or $1^1/_2$ teaspoons dried lemon grass, soaked in hot water until soft

5cm/2in piece fresh ginger, shredded

$^1/_2$ cup water

1 tablespoon vegetable oil

1 red onion, halved and sliced

2 fresh red chillies, sliced

2 tablespoons coconut vinegar

fresh coriander (cilantro) leaves

Method

1. Place mussels, coriander, lemon grass, ginger and water in a wok over a high heat. Cover and cook for 5 minutes or until mussels open. Discard any mussels that do not open after 5 minutes cooking. Remove mussels from wok, discard coriander, lemon grass and ginger. Strain cooking liquid and reserve.

2. Heat oil in a wok over a medium heat, add onion and chillies and stir-fry for 3 minutes or until onion is soft. Add mussels, reserved cooking liquid and coconut vinegar, and stir-fry for 2 minutes or until mussels are heated. Scatter with coriander leaves and serve.

Serves 4

Oyster Spring Rolls

Ingredients

2 tablespoons grated fresh ginger or shredded pickled ginger

1 tablespoon chopped fresh coriander (cilantro) or dill

1 tablespoon finely chopped chives or green onions

1 teaspoon lime or lemon juice

5 sheets spring roll pastry or 20 wonton wraps

20 fresh oysters, shucked, or 1 jar of about 20 oysters, drained

DIPPING SAUCE:

1 green onion, sliced diagonally

2 tablespoons rice wine vinegar

2 tablespoons reduced-salt soy sauce

1 tablespoon lime or lemon juice

Method

1. Preheat the oven to 180°C/350°F. Lightly spray or brush a baking tray with unsaturated oil.

2. Place ginger, coriander (cilantro) or dill, chives or green onions and lime juice in a small bowl. Mix to combine.

3. Cut each sheet of spring roll pastry into four squares. Place oyster on the centre of each square. Top with a little ginger mixture, brush edges with wate and fold in sides. Roll up.

4. Place rolls, seam side down, on the prepared baking tray. Bake for 10–12 minutes or until pastry is crisp and golden.

5. To make dipping sauce, place green onion, vinegar, soy sauce and lime or lemon juice in a small serving bowl. Mix to combine. When spring rolls are cooked, serve immediately with dipping sauce.

Makes 20 mini spring rolls

Pacific Rim Mussels

Ingredients

2 tablespoons vegetable oil

1 small onion, finely chopped

2 cloves garlic, crushed

1 teaspoon grated root ginger

1 teaspoon hot curry paste

$^1/_2$ teaspoon ground allspice

pinch cayenne pepper

400g/14oz can tomatoes, chopped

2 lime leaves, shredded

750mL/1$^2/_3$ lb large fresh mussels, scrubbed and cleaned and beards removed

salt and pepper

1 tablespoon chopped fresh coriander (cilantro), to garnish

Method

1. Heat oil in the bottom of a double boiler or large saucepan. Add onion, garlic, ginger, curry paste and allspice and cayenne pepper and fry gently for 10 minutes until softened.

2. Add chopped tomatoes and shredded lime leaves, cover and simmer for 20 minutes until thickened. Season to taste with salt and pepper.

3. Place mussels either in the top of the double boiler, or in a steamer set over the saucepan. Steam mussels over the sauce for 5 minutes. Discard any mussels do not open.

4. Carefully remove one half of each mussel shell, and arrange mussels in individual serving dishes. Spoon over the sauce, and serve at once garnished with coriander (cilantro).

Serves 6

Mussels Parquee

Ingredients

24 large, very fresh black mussels

1 Spanish onion, finely chopped

1 red chilli, finely chopped

$^2/_5$ cup aged red wine vinegar

55mL/2fl oz port wine

salt and pepper

lemon wedges

Method

1. Open mussels raw, using a small knife and the same technique as for opening oysters.

2. Mix all other ingredients together and set aside.

3. Put mussels on a serving platter, and top up with the onion mixture. Marinate for 5 minutes then serve icy cold with lemon wedges.

Serves 2

Mussels Parquee

Prawn Tostaditas

Ingredients

vegetable oil

8 corn tortillas

$^1/_2$ avocado, chopped

2 tablespoons shredded fresh mint

PRAWN AND VEGETABLE TOPPING:

1 cob sweet corn

1 red capsicum (pepper), quartered

1 yellow capsicum (pepper), quartered

2 teaspoons vegetable oil

1 red onion, cut into wedges

370g/13oz medium sized uncooked prawns, shelled and deveined

4 mild fresh green chillies, cut into strips

1 tablespoon lime juice

Method

1. To make topping, place sweet corn cob and red and yellow capsicums (peppers) on a preheated hot barbecue or char-grill and cook until lightly charred. Cut corn from cob and set aside. Cut capsicums (peppers) into strips and set aside.

2. Heat oil in a frying pan over a medium heat, add onion and cook for 4 minutes or until golden. Add prawns, chillies and lime juice and cook for 2 minutes or until prawns change colour. Add sweet corn kernels and red and yellow capsicums (peppers), toss to combine and set aside.

3. Heat $2^1/_2$cm/1in oil in a frying pan over a medium heat until a cube of bread dropped in browns in 50 seconds. Cook tortillas, one at time, for 45 seconds each side or until crisp. Drain on absorbent kitchen paper.

4. To serve, pile topping onto tortillas, then scatter with avocado and mint. Serve immediately.

Goan Curry with Pipies and Raita

Ingredients

GOAN CURRY

5mL/1½ fl oz oil

1 onion, finely sliced

2 cloves garlic, chopped

1 tablespoon cumin powder

1 tablespoon turmeric powder

2 tablespoons mild curry powder

1 tablespoon ginger powder

2 cardamom pods, cracked

1 pinch chilli powder

¼ stick cinnamon, cracked

½ cup water

500g/1 lb pipis, cleaned and sandless

500g/1 lb clams, cleaned and sandless

1½ cups coconut cream

1 tablespoon fresh chopped coriander (cilantro) leaves

RAITA:

½ cucumber peeled, centre removed and diced

1 tablespoon chopped fresh mint

5 tablespoons plain yoghurt

1 lemon, juiced

salt and pepper

Method

1. On medium heat in a large saucepan, add oil, onion, garlic and all spices, and cook for 2 minutes gently. Add shellfish and water, and cook until shellfish has opened. Stir frequently. As shellfish are opening, add coconut cream and coriander leaves.

2. To make raita, mix all ingredients together. Serve curry in a large bowl with Basmati rice and raita on the top.

exotic flavours

King Prawns in a Sweet Potato Crust

Ingredients

500g/1 lb large raw prawns, peeled and de-veined

MARINADE:

2 spring onions, finely chopped

1 stalk lemon grass, finely chopped

1 tablespoon fresh ginger, minced

1/2 bunch fresh coriander (cilantro), finely chopped

1 teaspoon Thai fish sauce (*nam pla*)

1 tablespoon sweet chilli sauce

2 tablespoons peanut oil

BATTER:

300g/10 1/2 oz sweet potato (kumara)

1/2 teaspoon turmeric

1 cup coconut milk

1/2 cup water

1/2 cup self-raising flour

1/2 cup rice flour

1 tablespoon polenta

Method

1. Chop prawns roughly and mix with spring onions, lemon grass, fresh ginger, coriander (cilantro), fish sauce and sweet chilli sauce. Allow to marinate for 1 hour.

2. Meanwhile, to make batter, grate the sweet potato. In a separate bowl, mix turmeric, coconut milk, water, self-raising flour, riceflour and polenta. Stir thoroughly to combine, then add grated sweet potato and set aside until prawns are ready. Combine prawn mixture with the batter and mix thoroughly.

3. Heat a nonstick fryingpan with peanut oil, and drop tablespoons of the prawn mixture into the fryingpan. Cook over a medium-high heat for 3 minutes on each side, or until the underside is crisp and golden. Turn them over and cook on the other side.

4. When cooked, remove the fritters from the fryingpan. Allow them to cool on a wire rack, or serve immediately with lime wedges. To reheat, place the wire rack in the oven, preheated to 200°C/400°F for 5–10 minutes.

Variation: If you do not wish to use shellfish, substitute fresh salmon for prawns and dice before mixing with the marinade. Then proceed with the recipe above. A combination of prawns and salmon also works very well.

Makes 12-16 fritters

Prawn Ceviche

Ingredients

500g/1 lb medium green prawns, shelled and deveined

3/4 cup lime juice

3/4 cup lemon juice

1/2 cup orange juice

1 fresh hot chilli, cut into strips

1 clove garlic, crushed

1 teaspoon brown sugar

1 red capsicum (pepper), cut into strips

1/2 small red onion, cut into strips

2 tablespoons fresh coriander (cilantro), chopped

2 ripe tomatoes, seeded and diced

salt and freshly ground black pepper

Method

1. In a bowl, marinate prawns in a mixture of the citrus juices, chilli, garlic and sugar for at least 6 hours or overnight. This marinade will 'cold cook' prawns, which should lose their translucent appearance.

2. Remove prawns from marinade and toss with remaining ingredients, seasoning well with salt and freshly ground black pepper.

Serves 2

Spanish Marinated Mussels

Ingredients

1 kg/2¼ lb mussels, cleaned, cooked *Mariniere* style and taken out of the shell (see page 237)

1 hard-boiled egg (white only), chopped finely

2 tablespoons baby capers

2 tablespoons fresh aromatic herbs, chopped (Thyme, rosemary, marjoram)

2 vine-ripened tomatoes, chopped finely

145mL/5fl oz Spanish virgin oil

1 tablespoon Dijon mustard

30mL/1fl oz old sherry vinegar

1 tablespoon fresh basil, roughly chopped

salt and pepper

Method

1. Mix all ingredients together and marinate in the refrigerator for 2 hours.

2. Before serving, put mussels bac< into their shells. Serve on a serving platter with a salad or as *Tapas* with glass of wine.

Serves 4

Mussels Tin Tin

Ingredients

1 kg/2¼ lb mussels, cleaned and beards removed

1 tablespoon peanut oil

55mL/2fl oz white wine

1 red chilli, sliced

1 stalk lemon grass, crushed

1 tablespoon fresh chopped ginger

1 clove garlic, chopped

100mL/3½ oz coconut cream

1 tablespoon fresh coriander, chopped

Method

1. Put white wine, chilli, lemon grass, ginger and garlic in a pot and infuse together for 15 minutes.

2. Put mussels in a casserole with oil, and add the infusion.

3. Add coconut cream and cook until mussels have opened, stirring frequently. Discard any mussels that do not open. Stir in coriander and serve.

Serves 4

Tiger Prawns with Oriental Dipping Sauce

Ingredients

1 tablespoon sunflower oil

10 green tiger prawns, shelled, deveined and tails intact

4 cos lettuce leaves

fresh coriander (cilantro) to garnish

ORIENTAL DIPPING SAUCE

1 clove garlic, crushed

$^1/_2$ teaspoon sugar

few drops of Tabasco sauce

finely grated rind and juice of $^1/_2$ lime

3 tablespoons sunflower oil

salt and ground black pepper

Method

1. To make dipping sauce, mix together all ingredients, and season to taste.

2. Heat oil in a frying pan, then fry prawns for 3–4 minutes or until pink and cooked through.

3. Arrange lettuce leaves on serving plates, scatter over prawns and garnish with coriander. Serve with dipping sauce.

Serves 2

Lemon Grass Prawns

Ingredients

1kg/2$^1/_4$ lb uncooked medium-sized prawns

3 stalks fresh lemon grass, finely chopped

2 spring onions, chopped

2 small fresh red chillies, finely chopped

2 cloves garlic, crushed

2 tablespoons finely grated fresh ginger

1 teaspoon shrimp paste

1 tablespoon brown sugar

$^1/_2$ cup coconut milk

Method

1. Wash prawns, leaving shells and heads intact, and place in a shallow glass or ceramic dish.

2. Place lemon grass, spring onions, chillies, garlic, ginger and shrimp paste in a food processor or blender and process until smooth. Add sugar and coconut mi k and process to combine. Spoon mixture over prawns, toss to combine, cover and marinate in the refrigerator for 3–4 hours.

3. Preheat the barbecue to a high heat. Drain prawns, place on the barbecue and cook, turning several times, for 5 minutes or until prawns change colour. Serve immediately.

Serves 4

Sake-Simmered Lobster

Ingredients

2 live lobsters, about 455g/1 lb each

2 leeks

115g/4oz watercress

8–10cm/3–4in fresh ginger 45g/$1\frac{1}{2}$ oz

1 tablespoon fresh ginger juice

chervil leaves

SIMMERING SAUCE:

$1\frac{3}{5}$ cups sake

$\frac{3}{4}$ cup water

7 tablespoons mirin

2 tablespoons dark soy sauce

2 tablespoons light soy sauce

2 tablespoons sugar

$\frac{1}{2}$ teaspoon salt

Method

1. Cut live lobsters in half lengthwise and then cut each half into 2–3 pieces.

2. Cut leeks into $1\frac{1}{2}$cm/$\frac{1}{2}$in rounds, boil in salted water until just tender, and drain.

3. Blanch watercress in lightly salted boiling water, drain, and refresh in cold water. Drain again and cut into 4cm/$1\frac{1}{2}$in lengths.

4. Slice ginger with the grain into very fine slivers and soak in cold water for 2–3 minutes.

5. To make simmering sauce, place sake and water in a saucepan and bring to a boil over high heat, then add all the remaining ingredients. Add lobster, and cover with a plate that fits down inside the pan and sits directly onto the food (this ensures even heat and flavour distribution by forcing the rising heat down). Boil for 5–6 minutes over high heat until the meat can be easily removed from the shell. Ladle simmering liquid over lobster several times. Add leek and watercress. Heat through, add the ginger juice, and remove immediately from heat.

6. Divide lobster and vegetables among 4 bowls. Pour in an ample amount of sauce. Top with well-drained ginger, garnish with chervil, and serve.

Serves 4

Curry Mussels

(opposite)

Ingredients

2 tablespoons olive oil

1 small onion, chopped

1 stick celery, sliced

1 clove garlic, chopped

2 tablespoons yellow curry paste

2 cardamom pods, crushed

1 pinch ground cumin

1kg/2 1/4 lb mussels, cleaned

55mL/2fl oz coconut cream

1 tablespoon fresh chopped coriander

1 red chilli, optional

Method

1. Put oil, onion, celery, garlic, curry paste, cardamom and cumin in a saucepan and cook over a slow heat for 5 minutes, stirring frequently.

2. Add mussels and coconut cream and increase heat to high.

3. Cook until all mussels have opened, stirring frequently to ensure mussels are cooked evenly. Discard any mussels that do not open.

4. Add coriander, stir and serve. Add chopped chilli if you like your curry very spicy.

Serves 4

Stir-Fried Tamarind Prawns

Ingredients

2 tablespoons tamarind pulp

$^{1}/_{2}$ cup water

2 teaspoons vegetable oil

3 stalks fresh lemon grass, chopped or 2 teaspoons finely grated lemon rind

2 fresh red chillies, chopped

500g/1 lb medium uncooked prawns, shelled and deveined with tails intact

2 green (unripe) mangoes, peeled and thinly sliced

3 tablespoons chopped fresh coriander (cilantro) leaves

2 tablespoons brown sugar

2 tablespoons lime juice

Method

1. Place tamarind pulp and water in a bowl and stand for 20 minutes. Strain, reserve liquid and set aside. Discard solids.

2. Heat oil in a wok or frying pan over a high heat, add lemon grass or lemonrind and chillies and stir-fry for 1 minute. Add prawns, and stir-fry for 2 minutes or until they change colour.

3. Add mangoes, coriander, sugar, lime juice and tamarind liquid, and stir-fry for 5 minutes or until prawns are cooked.

Serves 4

entertaining

Risotto of Chilli-Spiked Yabbies with Ginger

Ingredients

2 tablespoons peanut oil

1 brown onion, chopped

3 small fresh red chillies, minced

4cm piece fresh ginger or 2 teaspoons ground ginger

20 cooked yabbies, peeled

425g/15oz arborio rice

100mL/3½fl oz white wine

4 cups fish (or vegetable) stock, simmering

4 firm tomatoes, roughly chopped

3 shallots, sliced

2 tablespoons cream

saland pepper to taste

fresh sage leaves, fried until crisp

Method

1. Heat peanut oil in a large saucepan and add onion, chilli and ginger, sautéing for a 1–2 minutes or until onion has softened. Add the yabby meat and toss in onion and chilli mixture to coat. With a slotted spoon, remove yabbies and keep warm.

2. To onion and chilli mixture, add rice and stir to coat. Add white wine and allow the alcohol to be evaporated while the liquid is absorbed. Begin adding fish or vegetable stock, half a cup at a time, allowing each addition to be well absorbed before adding the next one. Stir well, often, to encourage the separation of starch from rice. When half the liquid has been absorbed, add chopped tomatoes and shallots, continuing adding stock as necessary.

3. When all the liquid has been added and rice is still slightly firm, add cream and salt and pepper to taste. Stir thoroughly and serve, garnished with crisp sage leaves.

Serves 4

Gratin of Crab

Ingredients

4 small crabs

1 tablespoon chopped shallots

½ cup chopped mushrooms

1 tablespoon butter or margarine

2 tablespoons Cognac

salt and pepper to taste

GRATIN SAUCE:

2 tablespoons butter or margarine

2 tablespoons flour

1½ cups fish stock

½ cup cream

1 teaspoon French mustard

1 teaspoon cayenne pepper

½ cup grated cheese

Method

1. Prepare crab meat in the usual way and set to one side, being careful to keep the shells intact.

2. Sauté shallots and mushrooms in butter or margarine, season and pour over warmed ignited Cognac. Remove from the heat.

3. Make gratinsauce by melting butter or margarine in a saucepan and stirring in flour over a low heat for 1–2 minutes. Gradually add fish stock, and stir until the sauce thickens, then stir in cream, mustard and cayenne pepper.

4. Allow sauce to simmer for 2–3 minutes, then remove from the heat and stir in crab meat and mushroom mixture.

5. Spoon sauce into crab shells, sprinkle with cheese and bake at 150°C/325°F for 5 minutes.

Serves 4

Bouillabaisse

Ingredients

3 kg/6 $^{2}/_{3}$lb mixed fish and seafood, including firm white fish fillets, prawns, mussels, crab and calamari rings

$^{1}/_{4}$ cup olive oil

2 cloves garlic, crushed

2 large onions, chopped

2 leeks, sliced

2 x 400g/14oz cans tomatoes, drained and mashed

1 tablespoon chopped fresh thyme or 1 teaspoon dried thyme

2 tablespoons chopped fresh basil or 1 $^{1}/_{2}$ teaspoons dried basil

2 tablespoons chopped fresh parsley

2 bay leaves

2 tablespoons finely grated orange rind

1 teaspoon saffron threads

1 cup dry white wine

1 cup fish stock

freshly ground black pepper

Method

1. Remove bones and skin from fish fillets and cut into 2cm/$^{3}/_{4}$in cubes. Peel and devein prawns, leaving tails intact. Scrub and remove beards from mussels. Cut crab into quarters. Set aside.

2. Heat oil in a large saucepan over a medium heat, add garlic, onions and leeks and cook for 5 minutes or until onions are golden. Add tomatoes, thyme, basil, parsley, bay leaves, orange rind, saffron, wine and stock and bring to the boil. Reduce heat and simmer for 30 minutes.

3. Add fish and crab and cook for 10 minutes. Add remaining seafood and cook for 5 minutes or until fish and seafood are cooked. Season to taste with freshly ground black pepper.

Serves 6

Lobster Mornay

Ingredients

1 medium lobster, cooked and halved

MORNAY SAUCE:

310mL/11oz milk

1 bay leaf

1 small onion, chopped

5 black peppercorns

30g/1oz butter

2 tablespoons plain flour

75mL/2½ fl oz cream

75g/2½ oz cheese, grated

salt and cracked black peppercorns

15g/½ oz butter, extra, melted

75g/2½ oz fresh breadcrumbs

Method

1. Remove lobster meat from shells and cut into bite-sized pieces. Reserve shells.

2. To make mornay sauce, in a saucepan, milk, bay leaf, onion and peppercorns. Heat slowly to boiling point. Remove from heat, cover and stand for 10 minutes. Strain.

3. In a pan, heat butter and remove from heat. Stir in flour and blend, gradually adding strained milk. Return the pan to the heat, and stir constantly (until sauce boils and thickens). Simmer sauce for 1 minute. Remove from heat, add cream, cheese, salt and pepper. Stir sauce until cheese melts, and add lobster.

4. Divide mixture between shells. Melt extra butter in a small saucepan, add breadcrumbs, and stir to combine.

5. Scatter buttered breadcrumbs over lobster and brown under a hot grill. Serve immediately.

Serves 2

Chilli Crab

Ingredients

2 medium or 1 large crab, or 6 blue swimmer crabs

3 tablespoons vegetable oil

1 tablespoon lemon juice

salt to taste

CHILLI SAUCE:

2 – 3 red chillies, seeded and chopped

1 onion, chopped

2 cloves garlic, chopped

2 teaspoons grated fresh ginger

2 tablespoons vegetable oil

2 ripe tomatoes, skinned, seeded and chopped, or 2 teaspoons tomato paste

1 teaspoon sugar

1 tablespoon light soy sauce

3 tablespoons water

Method

1. Clean crabs thoroughly, then cut each body into 2 or 4 pieces. Chop or crack the claws in 2 or 3 places if they are large. Heat oil in a frying pan, add crab pieces and fry for 5 minutes, stirring constantly. Add lemon juice and salt to taste, remove from the heat and keep hot.

2. To make sauce, put chillies, onion and garlic with ginger in a blender and work to a smooth paste. Heat oil in a wok or a deep frying pan. Add chilli paste and fry for 1 minute, stirring constantly. Add tomatoes ot tomato paste, sugar and soy sauce and stir-fry for 2 minutes, then stir in water. Add salt to taste and simmer for a further minute.

3. Add crab and stir to coat each piece in sauce. Cook crab for 1–2 minutes.
Serve hot.

Serves 4

Pipies in Black Bean

Ingredients

1 tablespoon sesame oil

1 kg/2 1/4 lb pipis cleaned and sand less

55mL/2fl oz water

115mL/4fl oz black bean sauce (see below)

1 tablespoon cornflour, mixed with 2 tablespoons water

1 tablespoon fresh coriander, chopped

3 spring onions, finely chopped

BLACK BEAN SAUCE:

4 tablespoons fermented black beans (also called salted black beans)

1 tablespoon fresh chopped ginger

1 red chilli, chopped

2 cloves garlic, chopped

1 tablespoon white vinegar

2 tablespoons soy sauce

1 pinch Chinese Five Spices

1 teaspoon sugar

2 tablespoons vegetable oil

Method

1. To make black bean sauce, rinse black beans thoroughly then mince (not rinsing beans will make the sauce too salty). Mix all sauce ingredients, and set aside for 15 minutes.

2. On high heat in a large saucepan, put sesame oil, pipis and water, and cook until pipis start to open. Add sauce and cook until all pipis have opened.

3. Add cornflour and stir until sauce has thickened, around 1 minute on high heat.

4. Add coriander and spring onions, and serve with rice or noodles.

Serves 4

Oysters Greta Garbo

Ingredients

3 dozen natural oysters in shells

juice of ½ lime or lemon

6 slices smoked salmon, cut into fine strips

1 cup sour cream

2 tablespoons fresh chives, chopped

red caviar

crushed ice

Method

1. Sprinkle oysters with lime or lemon juice, and top with smoked salmon.

2. Dollop sour cream onto each oyster.

3. Garnish with chives and red caviar. Serve on a bed of crushed ice.

Serves 6 as an entrée

Mexican Prawns in Salsa

Ingredients

750g/1 2/3lb uncooked large prawns, shelled and deveined

2 tablespoons lime juice

2 teaspoons ground cumin

2 tablespoons chopped fresh coriander (cilantro)

2 fresh red chillies, chopped

2 teaspoons vegetable oil

4 tortillas or flat bread

AVOCADO SALSA:

1 avocado, stoned, peeled and chopped

1 tablespoon lemon juice

1/2 red capsicum (pepper), chopped

2 spring onions, chopped

1/2 teaspoon chilli powder

1 tablespoon fresh coriander (cilantro) leaves

Method

1. Place prawns, lime juice, cumin, coriander (cilantro), chillies and oil in a bowl, toss to combine and set aside to marinate for 5 minutes.

2. To make salsa, place avocado, lemon juice, red capsicum (pepper), spring onions, chilli powder and coriander (cilantro) leaves in a bowl and mix gently to combine. Set aside.

3. Heat a nonstick frying pan over a high heat, add prawns and stir-fry for 4–5 minutes or until prawns are cooked. To serve, divide prawns among tortillas or flat bread and top with salsa.

Serves 4

Escargot Mussels

Ingredients

1kg/2¼ lb mussels, cooked mariniére style (see page 237)

GARLIC BUTTER:

500g/1 lb butter soft

2 cloves garlic, minced

1 tablespoon chopped fresh parsely

30mL/1fl oz brandy

salt and pepper

Method

1. Remove the extra half shell of mussels and keep the mussel in one shell.

2. To make garlic butter, mix all ingredients together until smooth.

3. Top up mussels in half shell with garlic butter. Grill mussels until sizzling. Serve with bread or chips on the side.

Serves 6 as an entrée

Lobster Newburg

Ingredients

60g butter

2kg/4$^{1}/_{2}$ lb lobster (cooked, shelled and cut into small pieces)

2 teaspoons salt

$^{1}/_{4}$ teaspoon cayenne pepper

$^{1}/_{4}$ teaspoon nutmeg

1 cup double cream

4 egg yolks

2 tablespoons brandy

2 tablespoons dry sherry

reserved lobster-tail shell or 4-6 vol-au-vent cases and rice (for serving)

Method

1. In a shallow fryingpan, melt butter over a moderate heat. When the foam subsides, add lobster and cook slowly for about 5 minutes. Add the salt, cayenne pepper and nutmeg.

2. In a small bowl lightly beat cream with egg yolks. Add the mixture to the frying pan, stirring continuously.

3. Then add brandy and sherry. Do not allow to boil as the sauce will curdle.

5. Serve either placed back in the lobster tail shell, or in vol-au-vent cases. Serve with steamed rice in shell or vol-au-vent cases.

Serves 4 – 6

Grilled Scampi with Herb Butter

Ingredients

12 scampi

125g/4½ oz butter

few sprigs fresh herbs, chopped

2 tablespoons chopped parsley

2 cloves garlic, chopped finely

freshly ground pepper

Method

1. Split scampi lengthwise through the centre and arrange cut side up in a large shallow dish.

2. Melt butter and add the herbs and garlic. Drizzle the herb butter over the scampi and season with freshly ground pepper. The scampi can be prepared ahead up to this stage.

3. Preheat the griller and arrange scampi, cut side up, on the grilling tray. Cook for about 5 minutes until the flesh has turned white. Remove from heat, season with salt and arrange on a large serving platter with wedges of lemon.

4. To eat the scampi use a fork to pull out the tail meat. Place a bowl on the table for the discarded shells.

Serves 4 as an entrée

Coconut Prawns and Scallops

Ingredients

1kg/2¼lb large uncooked prawns, shelled, deveined and tails left intact

3 egg whites, lightly beaten

85g/3oz shredded coconut

vegetable oil for deep-frying

1 tablespoon peanut oil

4 fresh red chillies, seeded and sliced

2 small fresh green chillies, seeded and sliced

2 cloves garlic, crushed

1 tablespoon shredded fresh ginger

3 kaffir lime leaves, finely shredded

370g/13oz scallops

115g/4oz snow pea (*mangetout*) leaves or sprouts

2 tablespoons palm or brown sugar

¼ cup lime juice

2 tablespoons Thai fish sauce (*nam pla*)

Method

1. Dip prawns in egg whites, then roll in coconut to coat. Heat vegetable oil in a large saucepan until a cube of bread dropped in browns in 50 seconds. Cook prawns, a few at a time, for 2–3 minutes or until golden and crisp. Drain on absorbent kitchen paper and keep warm.

2. Heat peanut oil in a wok over a high heat, add red and green chillies, garlic, ginger and lime leaves, and stir-fry for 2–3 minutes or until fragrant.

3. Add scallops to the wok and stir-fry for 3 minutes or until opaque. Add cooked prawns, snow pea (mangetout) leaves or sprouts, sugar, lime juice and fish sauce and stir-fry for 2 minutes or until heated. serve immediately.

Serves 6

Thai Garlic Prawns

Ingredients

6 cloves garlic, crushed

6 tablespoons chopped fresh coriander

3 tablespoons vegetable oil

500g/1 lb uncooked large prawns, shelled, deveined and tails left intact

$^3/_4$ cup water

$^1/_4$ cup Thai fish sauce (*nam pla*)

1 tablespoon sugar

freshly ground black pepper

Method

1. Place garlic, coriander and 2 tablespoons oil in a food processor or blender and process until smooth.

2. Heat remaining oil in a large wok or frying pan, add garlic mixture and stir-fry for 2 minutes. Add prawns and stir-fry to coat with garlic mixture. Stir in water, fish sauce, sugar and black pepper to taste and stir-fry until prawns are cooked. Serve immediately.

Serves 4

Dijon Mussels

Ingredients

30g/1oz butter

$^1/_2$ onion, finely chopped

$^1/_2$ bunch celery, finely chopped

$^1/_2$ leek, finely chopped

1kg/2$^1/_4$ lb mussels, cleaned

1 cup dry white wine

1 cup cream

1 tablespoon Dijon mustard

pepper

1 tablespoon chopped parsley

Method

1. On a high heat in a saucepan, melt butter and add onion, celery and leek and cook for 1 minute. Add mussels and white wine, and cover.

2. Mix cream and mustard together, and add to the saucepan with pepper to taste.

3. Stir frequently to ensure even cooking of mussels. When mussels have opened, add parsley. Discard any mussels that do not open, and serve.

Serves 4

Fried Vongole

Ingredients

salt and pepper to taste

2 eggs, beaten

1kg/2¼ lb pipies cleaned, cooked mariniére style and removed from shell (see page 327)

2 cups bread crumbs

1 tablespoon dry mixed aromatic herbs

vegetable oil for frying

3 tablespoons tartare sauce

2 eggs, beaten

Method

1. Add salt and pepper to taste to beaten eggs. Add pipis to the egg mixture

2. Mix breadcrumbs and dry herbs. Roll pipis in breadcrumbs and shake to remove excess.

3. Deep-fry pipis in oil for a few minutes until golden brown. Drain on absorbent paper and serve immediately in their shells with tartare sauce and lemon wedges.

Serves 6 as an entreé

Lobster Provençale

Ingredients

55g/2oz butter

1 teaspoon freshly crushed garlic

2 spring onions, chopped

310g/11oz can tomatoes

salt and cracked black peppercorns to taste

pinch saffron

1 large lobster cooked

55mL/2oz brandy

boiled rice

½ bunch fresh chives, chopped

lemon wedges

Method

1. In a shallow fryingpan melt butter over a moderate heat. Add garlic, spring onions, tomatoes, salt and pepper, and saffron. Cook until onions are translucent about 2 minutes.

2. Remove meat from lobster, and cut into large pieces. Add lobster to the frying pan, and flame with brandy. Cook gently until lobster is heated through.

3. Place rice on a serving plate, and sprinkle with chives.

4. Remove lobster from the fryingpan, retaining the cooking liquid as a sauce. Arrange lobster on rice, and spoon the sauce over lobster. Serve with lemon wedges.

Serves 4

Griddled Scallops with Orange Salsa

Ingredients

2 small oranges

4 sun-dried tomatoes in oil, drained and chopped

1 clove garlic, crushed

1 tablespoon balsamic vinegar

4 tablespoons extra virgin olive oil

salt and black pepper

1 large head fennel, cut lengthways into 8 slices

12 fresh scallops

4 tablespoons crème fraîche

rocket leaves

Method

1. Slice the top and bottom off 1 orange, then cut away the peel and pith, following the curve of the fruit. Cut between the membranes to release the segments, then chop roughly. Squeeze the juice of second orange into a bowl, add chopped orange, tomatoes, garlic, vinegar and 3 tablespoons of the oil, then season to taste and set aside.

2. Heat a ridged cast-iron grill pan or heavy-based frying pan. Brush both sides of each fennel slice with half remaining oil. Cook for 2 – 3 minutes on each side, until tender and charred. Transfer to serving plates and keep warm.

3. Brush scallops with remaining oil and cook for 1 minute, then turn and cook for 30 seconds or until cooked through. Top fennel with 1 tablespoon crème fraîche, 3 scallops and the salsa. Serve with rocket.

Serves 4

Seafood Pâté

Ingredients

500g/1 lb trout fillets, skinned and boned

500g/1 lb uncooked prawns, shelled and deveined

85g/3oz butter

4 spring onions, chopped

2 cloves garlic, crushed

2 tablespoons brandy

2 tablespoons chopped fresh dill

$^1/_2$ cup double cream

1 tablespoon lemon juice

2 teaspoons chilli sauce

freshly ground black pepper

fresh dill sprigs

melba toasts or cracker biscuits

Method:

1. Coarsely chop trout and prawns and set aside.

2. Melt butter in a saucepan over a medium heat, add spring onions and garlic and cook, stirring, for 1 minute or until onions are soft. Add trout and prawns and cook, stirring, until seafood is just cooked. Add brandy and cook for 1 minute, then stir in dill, cream, lemon juice and chilli sauce. Remove the sauce pan from the heat and set aside to cool.

3. Transfer mixture to a food processor, season to taste with black pepper and process until smooth. Spoon mixture into a serving dish, cover and refrigerate for at least 6 hours. To serve, garnish pâté with dill sprigs and accompany with melba toasts or cracker biscuits.

Serves 8

Butterflied Prawns

Ingredients

500g/1 lb green king prawns

1 ham steak

1 zucchini (courgette)

6 shallots

2 tablespoons vegetable oil

1 chicken stock cube, crumbled

2 tablespoons cornflour, blended with a little water

2 tablespoons sherry

2 tablespoons soy sauce

Method

1. Shell and devein prawns, leaving tails intact. Make a shallow cut along back of each prawn. Cut a 1cm/½in slit right through the centre of each prawn.

2. Cut ham, zucchini (courgette) and shallots into thin straws, 5cm/2in long. Push a piece of each through the slit in each prawn.

3. Heat oil in a wok or frying pan, add prawns and stir-fry for 1 minute.

4. Stir in blended cornflour, water, stock cube, sherry and soy sauce and stir over heat until the mixture boils and thickens. Remove prawns and put on a serving platter. Reserve cooking mixture, and use as a dipping sauce for prawns.

Makes 24

Lobster in Mint Pesto

Ingredients

2 uncooked lobster tails, halved lengthwise

MINT PESTO:

1 bunch fresh mint

4 tablespoons almonds, toasted

1 clove garlic, crushed

$^1/_4$ cup lime juice

$^1/_4$ cup olive oil

Method

1. To make pesto, place mint leaves, almonds, garlic and lime juice in a food processor or blender and process. With the machine running, slowly add oil and make a smooth paste.

2. Place lobster on a baking tray, spread flesh with pesto and bake for 15–20 minutes at 200°C/400°F or until lobster is cooked.

Serving suggestion: This dish is perfect for a special occasion meal. Start with an antipasto platter; purchase the ingredients from the delicatessen section of your supermarket. Accompany lobster with boiled new potatoes tossed with olive oil and black pepper and a salad of assorted lettuces and chopped fresh herbs. Finish the meal with a good quality purchased ice cream topped with a tablespoon of your favourite liqueur.

Serves 4

Mussels Riviera

Ingredients

1kg/2¼ lb mussels cleaned, cooked and removed in half shell

1 tablespoon olive oil

1 onion, chopped finely

2 cloves garlic, chopped

4 tomatoes, chopped finely

½ red capsicum (pepper), chopped finely

200mL/7fl oz white wine

2 tablespoons rosemary, thyme and basil mix, dry or freshly chopped

salt, pepper and paprika

1 tablespoon grated Parmesan cheese

Method

1. Cook mussels mariniére style and remove 1 shell from each mussel (see page 237).

2. Heat oil in a saucepan, and add onion, garlic, tomatoes and red capsicum (capsicum). Cook for 5 minutes.

3. Add white wine and herbs, season with salt, pepper and paprika; cook slowly for 30 minutes until mixture reaches a paste consistency.

4. Using a spoon, cover mussels with the paste, top up with Parmesan cheese and grill.

5. Serve on a plater with foccacia bread.

Serves 4 as an entreé

Spaghettini and Scallops with Breadcrumbs

Ingredients

12 fresh scallops with their corals

$^1/_2$ cup extra virgin olive oil

55g/2oz dried white breadcrumbs

4 tablespoons chopped fresh flat-leaf parsley

2 cloves garlic, finely chopped

1 teaspoon crushed dried chillies

340g/12oz dried spaghettini

salt

4 tablespoons dry white wine

Method

1. Detach corals from scallops and set aside. Slice each white part into 3 or 4 pieces. Heat 2 tablespoons oil in a frying pan, then add breadcrumbs and fry, stirring, for 3 minutes or until golden. Remove from the fryingpan and set aside.

2. Heat 5 tablespoons oil in the frying pan, then add 2 tablespoons parsley, garlic and chillies and fry for 2 minutes or until their flavours are released. Meanwhile, cook spaghettini in plenty of boiling salted water, until tender but still firm to the bite. Drain, return to the saucepan and toss with remaining oil.

3. Stir the white parts of scallops into the frying pan and fry for 30 seconds or until starting to turn opaque. Add wine and the reserved scallop corals, cook for 30 seconds, then addspaghettini and cook for 1 minute, tossing to combine. Sprinkle with breadcrumbs and remaining parsley.

Serves 4

Spinach Mornay Mussels

Ingredients

1kg/2¼lb mussels, cleaned

2 tablespoons butter

3 tablespoons flour

1⅗ cups milk

200g/7oz grated Cheddar cheese

55g/2oz Parmesan cheese

225g/8oz baby spinach

salt, pepper, nutmeg

Method

1. Cook mussels mariniére style (see page 237) and remove 1 shell from each mussel.

2. Melt butter slowly in a saucepan, taking car that the butter does not brown. Add flour and mix until very smooth, using a wooden spatula.Add milk with a whisk and put back on the heat, stir with the whisk until boiling. Reduce heat and cook slowly for 5 minutes.

3. Add cheeses (Cheddar and Parmesan) and seasonings. Cook for another 5 minutes on a low heat, until cheeses have completely melted. Stir in baby spinach.

4. Top up the shell mussels with the spinach Mornay sauce and grill until golden brown.

Serves 4 as an entreé

Grilled Oysters with Champagne and Cream

Ingredients

12 fresh oysters

3 tablespoons champagne or dry sparkling wine

30g/1oz butter

2 tablespoons double cream

black pepper

115g/4oz baby spinach

Method

1. Open oysters, and scoop out each oyster with a teaspoon. Strain the liquor into a small saucepan. Remove and discard the muscle from 12 rounded half-shells, then wash and dry. Place in a flameproof dish lined with crumpled foil so that they sit level.

2. Bring the liquor to a simmer and poach oysters for 30–60 seconds, until just firm. Remove from the saucepan. Add champagne or dry sparkling wine to the saucepan and boil for 2 minutes to reduce. Remove from the heat and whisk in butter, then cream. Season with pepper.

3. Preheat the grill to high. Cook spinach in a saucepan for 2–3 minutes, until wilted. Squeeze out the excess liquid and divide between the shells. Top with an oyster and spoon over a little sauce. Cook close to the grill for 1 minute or until heated through.

Serves 4

Grilled Lobster with Chilli Salsa

Ingredients

2 cooked lobsters, about 340g/12oz each

4 teaspoons olive oil

cayenne pepper

SALSA:

2 tablespoons olive oil

1 red capsicum (pepper), deseeded and diced

1 small onion, chopped

1 large red chilli, deseeded and finely chopped

1 tablespoon sun-dried tomato purée

salt and black pepper

Method

1. To make salsa, heat oil in a saucepan and fry red capsicum (pepper), onion and chilli for 5 minutes or until tender. Stir in the tomato purée and season to taste. Transfer to a bowl.

2. To cut lobsters in half lengthways, turn one on its back. Cut through the head end first, using a large, sharp knife, then turn lobster round and cut through the tail end. Discard the small greyish 'sac' in the head; everything else in the shell is edible. Crack the large claws with a small hammer or wooden rolling pin. Repeat with the second lobster. Drizzle the cut side of lobsters with oil and sprinkle with cayenne pepper.

3. Heat a large non-stick frying pan or ridged cast-iron grill pan until very hot, then add lobster halves, cut-side down, and cook for 2–3 minutes, until lightly golden. Serve with salsa.

Serves 2

light meals

Spring Roll Baskets

Ingredients

vegetable oil for deep-frying

8 spring roll or wonton wrappers, each $12^1/_2$ cm/5in square

2 tablespoons unsalted cashews, toasted

PORK AND PRAWN FILLING:

1 tablespoon peanut (groundnut) oil

2 teaspoons finely grated fresh ginger

1 small fresh red chilli, finely chopped

4 spring onions, finely chopped

250g/$8^1/_2$ oz lean pork mince

115g/4oz uncooked prawns, shelled and deveined

1 tablespoon soy sauce

2 teaspoons Thai fish sauce

2 teaspoons honey

2 teaspoons lemon juice

30g/1oz bean sprouts

1 small carrot, cut into thin strips

1 tablespoon finely chopped fresh coriander

Method

1. Heat vegetable oil in a large saucepan until a cube of bread dropped in browns in 50 seconds. Place 2 spring roll or wonton wrappers, diagonally, one on top of the other, so that the corners are not matching. Shape wrappers around the base of a small ladle, lower into hot oil and cook for 3–4 minutes. During cooking keep wrappers submerged in oil by pushing down with the ladle to form a basket shape. Drain on absorbent kitchen paper. Repeat with remaining wrappers to make 4 baskets.

2. To make filling, heat peanut (groundnut) oil in a frying pan, add ginger, chilli and spring onions and stir-fry for 1 minute. Add pork and stir-fry for 5 minutes or until meat is brown. Add prawns, soy sauce, fish sauce, honey, lemon juice, bean sprouts, carrot and coriander and stir-fry for 4–5 minutes longer or until prawns change colour.

3. To serve, spoon filling into baskets and sprinkle with cashews.

Serves 4

Lemon-Scented Fish Pie

Ingredients

1kg/2¹/₄ lb potatoes, cut into even-sized pieces

55g/2oz butter

1 onion, chopped

2 stalks celery, sliced

2 tablespoons plain flour

1 cup fish stock

finely grated rind and juice of 1 large lemon

salt and black pepper

455g/1 lb cod or other white fish, cut into cubes

170g/6oz mussels, cooked and shelled

2 tablespoons chopped fresh parsley

4 tablespoons milk

Method

1. Cook potatoes in boiling salted water for 15–20 minutes or until tender, then drain.

2. Meanwhile, melt 30g/1oz of butter in a large saucepan, then add onion and celery and cook for 2–3 minutes or until softened. Add flour and cook, stirring, for 1 minute, then slowly add fish stock and cook, stirring, until thickened. Add lemon rind and juice and season with pepper.

3. Preheat the oven to 220°C/425°F. Remove the sauce from the heat, stir in cod, mussels and parsley, then transfer to an ovenproof dish. Mash potatoes with remaining butter and milk. Season, then spread evenly over the fish with a fork. Cook in the oven for 30–40 minutes, until the sauce is bubbling and the topping is starting to brown.

Serves 4

Clams with Pasta

Ingredients

2 tablespoons olive oil

1 large onion, finely chopped

1 clove garlic, minced

1 red capsicum (pepper), finely chopped

1 medium tomato, skinned, seeded and finely chopped

1 tablespoon minced parsley

1 bay leaf

few strands saffron

salt

freshly ground pepper

200g/7oz spaghetti, broken into three lengths

1/2 cup veal broth, or a mixture of chicken and beef broth

24 very small clams

3 tablespoons fresh or frozen peas

salt and pepper to taste

Method

1. Heat 1 tablespoon of oil in a frying pan, saute onion, garlic and capsicum (pepper) for 1 minute, then cover and cook slowly until the vegetables are tender but not brown, about 20 minutes. Add tomato, parsley, bay leaf, saffron, salt and pepper to the onion mixture and cook for 5 minutes, uncovered.

2. Bring a large saucepan of salted water to boil with remaining tablespoon of oil. Add spaghetti and cook, stirring occasionally with a fork. While spaghetti is still cooking, add onion and tomato mixture to the saucepan in which the spaghetti is cooking. Add 1/4 cup of broth, clams and peas. Mix well. Cover and continue cooking until clams have opened, about 10 minutes.

3. To serve, add remaining 1/4 cup broth (the mixture should be a little soupy) and taste for salt and pepper – it should be well seasoned. Serve in small individual casserole dishes. Although best prepared at the last minute, this dish can be made in advance and reheated.

Serves 8

Mussel and Zucchini Gratin

Ingredients

2kg/4$^{1}/_{2}$ lb mussels, cleaned and beards removed

$^{1}/_{2}$ cup finely chopped shallots

1 bay leaf

$^{2}/_{3}$ cup dry white wine

1kg/2$^{1}/_{4}$ lb zucchini (courgette), sliced

salt and freshly ground pepper

$^{1}/_{4}$ cup olive oil

1$^{1}/_{4}$ cups cream

3 egg yolks

2 tablespoons grated gruyere cheese

Method

1. Place mussels in a large saucepan with shallots and bay leaf, cover and cook over a brisk heat for 5 minutes or until the shells have opened. Remove mussels with a slotted spoon.

2. Taste the cooking liquid, and if too salty, discard half. Add wine to the saucepan and reduce the liquid to about $^{1}/_{2}$ cup, strain and reserve. Shell mussels, and if they are large discard the black rims, set them aside.

3. Wash, trim and slice zucchini. Season zucchini with salt and pepper, and sauté gently in olive oil in a large frying pan until lightly browned. Transfer to a large gratin dish.

4. Reduce 1 cup of cream over a gentle heat to $^{3}/_{4}$ cup and stir in the reserved mussel cooking liquor. In a small bowl, beat egg yolks with remaining cream and stir in 2 tablespoons of hot reduced cream mixture. Stir this mixture into the cream sauce in the saucepan, then remove from the heat. Taste for seasoning.

5. Top zucchini with mussels, then the cream sauce. Sprinkle with cheese and heat in a preheated hot oven (225°C /425°F) for 10 minutes, or until the top is browned.

Serves 4

Grilled Salmon Steaks with Mint Vinaigrette

Ingredients

4 salmon steaks, about 170g/6oz each

salt and black pepper

MINT VINAIGRETTE:

2 tablespoons chopped fresh mint

1 small shallot, finely chopped

6 tablespoons olive or vegetable oil

juice of 1 lemon

extra mint leaves to garnish

Method

1. Preheat the grill to high and line the grill tray with kitchen foil. Place salmon steaks on top and season lightly. Grill for 4–5 minutes on each side, until lightly browned and cooked through.

2. To make vinaigrette, mix together mint, shallot, oil and lemon juice, then season to taste. Spoon over salmon steaks and garnish with extra mint.

Serves 4

Scallop and Prawn Sticks

Ingredients

6 uncooked king prawns, shelled and deveined

500g/1 lb scallops

1 large onion, cut into eighths

6 bamboo skewers, soaked in water for 30 minutes

MARINADE:

1 tablespoon olive oil

2 tablespoons white wine

2 teaspoons finely chopped fresh dill

2 teaspoons finely chopped fresh parsley

2 teaspoons finely chopped fresh chives

2 cloves garlic, crushed

2 teaspoons grated lime rind

2 tablespoons lime juice

freshly ground black pepper

Method

1. Thread prawns, scallops and onions onto bamboo skewers.

2. To make marinade, combine oil, wine, dill, parsley, chives, garlic, lime rind and juice in a glass dish. Season to taste with pepper. Add skewered seafood and marinate for 1 hour.

3. Remove seafood from marinade and grill for 2–3 minutes on each side, turning and brushing with marinade frequently. Serve immediately.

Serves 6

Beef with Prawns and Noodles

Ingredients

145g/5oz rice noodles

1 tablespoon peanut (groundnut) oil

2 cloves garlic, crushed

250g/8$^{1}/_{2}$ oz lean beef mince

250g/8$^{1}/_{2}$ oz uncooked prawns, shelled and deveined

2 tablespoons castor sugar

2 tablespoons white vinegar

1 tablespoon Thai fish sauce (*nam pla*)

1 fresh red chilli, finely chopped

2 eggs, lightly beaten

115g/4oz bean sprouts

1 large carrot, grated

3 tablespoons chopped fresh coriander

2 tablespoons chopped blanched almonds

Method

1. Place noodles in a bowl, pour over boiling water to cover and set aside to stand for 8 minutes. Drain well.

2. Heat oil and garlic in a wok or large frying pan over a high heat, add beef and stir-fry for 2–3 minutes or until meat is brown. Add prawns and stir-fry for 1 minute. Stir in sugar, vinegar, fish sauce, and chilli and bring to the boil, stirring constantly.

3. Add eggs to the wok or frying pan, and cook, stirring, until set. Add bean sprouts, carrot and noodles and toss to combine. To serve, sprinkle with coriander (cilantro) and almonds.

Serves 4

Sour Prawns Curry

Ingredients

2 cups coconut milk

1 teaspoon shrimp paste

2 tablespoons Thai green curry paste

1 stalk fresh lemon grass, finely chopped or 1/2 teaspoon dried lemon grass, soaked in hot water until soft

2 fresh green chillies, chopped

1 tablespoon ground cumin

1 tablespoon ground coriander

500g/1 lb uncooked large prawns, shelled and deveined with tails left on

3 cucumbers, halved and sliced

115g/4oz can bamboo shoots, drained

1 tablespoon tamarind concentrate, dissolved in 3 tablespoons hot water

Method

1. Place coconut milk, shrimp paste, curry paste, lemon grass, chillies, cumin and coriander in a wok and bring to simmering point over a medium heat. Simmer, stirring occasionally, for 10 minutes.

2. Stir prawns, cucumbers, bamboo shoots and tamarind mixture into coconut milk mixture, and cook, stirring occasionally, for 5 minutes or until prawns are cooked.

Serves 4

Stir-Fried Chilli Prawns

Ingredients

1 teaspoon vegetable oil

1 teaspoon sesame oil

3 cloves garlic, crushed

3 fresh red chillies, chopped

1kg/2$^1/_4$ lb uncooked medium prawns, shelled and deveined

1 tablespoon brown sugar

$^1/_3$ cup tomato juice

1 tablespoon soy sauce

rocket leaves

Method

1. Heat vegetable and sesame oils together in a wok over a medium heat, add garlic and chillies and stir-fry for 1 minute. Add prawns and stir-fry for 2 minutes or until they change colour.

2. Stir in sugar, tomato juice and soy sauce, and stir-fry for 3 minutes or until sauce is heated through. Serve immediately with rocket leaves.

Serves 4

Seafood Risotto

Ingredients

500g/1 lb assorted seafood, such as prawns, calamari and scallops

500g/1 lb white fish fillets such as blue eye, boneless

2 tablespoons olive oil

2 cloves garlic, crushed

1/4 – 1/2 teaspoon minced chilli

1 tablespoon olive oil

2 onions, sliced

400g/14oz arborio rice

200mL/7fl oz white wine

2 bay leaves

2 stalks celery, sliced

2 large tomatoes, chopped

3 cups rich fish stock, simmering

1/2 cup milk or hot taco sauce

2 potatoes, peeled and diced

100mL/3 1/2 oz cream

1 bunch parsley, chopped

2 potatoes, boiled and thinl sliced

1 teaspoon paprika

Method

1. Prepare shellfish, and cut fish fillets into 2 1/2cm/1in chunks.

2. Heat the olive oil in a large saucepan and sauté garlic, chilli and fish chunks until opaque. Remove with a slotted spoon and keep warm. Add shellfish to the same saucepan and sauté until just cooked and changed colour, about 3 minutes. Remove the saucepan from the heat, return fish and mix gently. Set aside.

2. In another large saucepan, heat olive oil and sauté onions. Add rice and stir to coat, allowing rice to become translucent. Add wine and allow to simmer until the liquid evaporates. Add the bay leaves, diced potato and celery with the first addition of 1/2 cup of stock. Stir vigorously to combine. When stock has been absorbed, add the next 1/2 cup of stock. Continue in this fashion, adding stock and stirring thoroughly until the last quantity of stock is added.

3. Add chopped tomatoes, milk or taco sauce, cream and 1/2 bunch parsley. When all the ingredients have been added and most of stock has been absorbed, remove pan from the heat, remove the bay leaves and serve in individual bowls on a bed of boiled sliced potatoes, garnished with parsley and a sprinkling of paprika.

Serves 6

Chilli-Spiked Mussels in Spaghetti

Ingredients

340g/12oz dried spaghetti

1kg/2 1/4 lb fresh mussels, cleaned and beards removed

2 tablespoon olive oil

2 shallots, finely chopped

4 cloves garlic, chopped

3/5 cup dry white wine

grated rind of 1/2 lemon

1/2 teaspoon dried chilli flakes

2 tablespoons chopped fresh parsley

black pepepr to taste

Method

1. Cook spaghetti according to the packet instructions, until tender but still firm to the bite, then drain well.

2. Place mussels in a large heavy-based saucepan, with just the water clinging to the shell from cleaning. Steam for 3–4 minutes over a high heat, shaking regularly, until the shells have opened. Discard any mussels that remain closed.

3. Heat olive oil in a large saucepan and gently fry shallots and garlic for 5 minutes or until softened. Add wine and boil rapidly for 5–6 minutes, until the liquid has reduced by half. Add the mussels, lemon rind and chilli and heat for 2–3 minutes. Add the spaghetti to mussels, then stir in parsley and black pepper to taste. Gently toss over the heat and serve immediately.

Serves 4

Clams Provençale

Ingredients

$^{2}/_{5}$ cup virgin olive oil

1 onion, finely chopped

1 red capsicum (pepper), diced

4 vine-ripened tomatoes, diced

$^{1}/_{2}$ stalk celery, sliced

2 cloves garlic, chopped

1kg/2$^{1}/_{4}$ lb surf clams, cleaned and sandless

$^{3}/_{5}$ cup dry white wine

1 tablespoon freshly chopped aromatic herbs (thyme, rosemary, marjoram)

salt and pepper

Method

1. On high heat in a large saucepan, put oil, onion, red capsicum (pepper), tomatoes, celery, garlic and cook for 5 minutes, stirring occasionally to avoid sticking.

2. Add surf clams, white wine, fresh herbs and seasoning and cook covered until all shells have opened. Stir frequently to ensure evenly cooking.

3. When clams are open, serve in large bowls with a salad or grilled baguette, and complement the dish with a rose or white wine.

Serves 4

Prawns with Coriander Butter

(opposite)

Ingredients

750g/1¼lb large king prawns, shelled and deveined with tails intact

¼ cup olive oil

1 bunch coriander (cilantro)

2 cloves garlic, crushed

salt to taste

2 tablespoons lemon juice

¼ cup each of dry white wine and dry vermouth

1 tablespoon white wine vinegar

2 tablespoons spring onions, chopped

85g/3oz butter

a little lemon juice

salt and pepper)

225g/8oz snow peas (mangetout)

½ red capsicum (pepper), cut into thin strips

115g/4oz oriental or button mushrooms

Method

1. Marinate prawns for a few hours in oil, ½ bunch coriander (cilantro) sprigs, garlic, salt and lemon juice.

2. To coriander butter, place wine, vermouth, vinegar and spring onions into a saucepan. Bring to the boil and reduce to about 3 tablespoons. Over a little heat, whisk in butter in small pieces until the sauce thickens. Season with a little lemon juice, salt and pepper. Chop remaining coriander (cilantro) and stir into butter sauce.

3. Heat a large frying pan and sauté prawns for about 2 minutes. At the same time have a saucepan of boiling salted water ready and drop in snow peas (mangetout), red capsicum (pepper) and mushrooms for 1 minute.

4. Drain and toss vegetables with the prawns in the frying pan. Divide prawns among 4 plates, reheat the sauce and spoon over each serving.

Serves 4

Prawn Toast

Ingredients

500g/1 lb peeled cooked prawns, deveined

6 spring onions, chopped

2 teaspoons grated fresh root ginger

2 teaspoons light soy sauce

1/2 teaspoon sesame oil

2 egg whites

6 slices white bread

30g/1oz fresh white breadcrumbs

oil for deep-frying

Method

1. Combine prawns, spring onions, ginger, soy sauce and sesame oil in a blender or food processor. Blend until roughly chopped. Add egg whites and blend until combined.

2. Remove crusts from bread slices, spread them with prawn mixture, then cut each slice into 3 strips.

3. Dip prawn-coated side of each bread strip into breadcrumbs. Deep-fry bread strips in hot oil until light golden brown. Drain on absorbant kitchen paper and serve at once.

Makes 18

Singapore Noodles

Ingredients

500g/1 lb fresh egg noodles

2 teaspoons vegetable oil

2 eggs, lightly beaten

1 teaspoon sesame oil

1 onion, chopped

1 red capsicum (pepper), chopped

2 cloves garlic, crushed

1 fresh red chilli, chopped

8 uncooked large prawns, shelled and deveined

255g/9oz Chinese barbecued pork or Chinese roast pork, thinly sliced

6 spring onions, sliced

2 tablespoons fresh coriander leaves

1 teaspoon sugar

1 teaspoon ground turmeric

1/2 teaspoon ground cumin

2 tablespoons soy sauce

Mothod

1. Place noodles in a bowl of boiling water and stand for 5 minutes. Drain and set aside.

2. Heat vegetable oil in a wok over a medium heat, add eggs and swirl around thewok to coat base and sides. Cook for 2 minutes or until set. Remove omelette from the wok, cool, then roll up and cut into thin strips.

3. Heat sesame oil in a clean wok over a high heat, add onion, red capsicum (pepper), garlic and chilli and stir-fry for 3 minutes. Add prawns and pork and stir-fry for 3 more minutes.

4. Add noodles, egg strips, spring onions, coriander, sugar, turmeric, cumin and soy sauce to the wok and stir-fry for 3 minutes or until heated through. Serve immediately.

Serves 4

Fresh Crab Tagliatelle

Ingredients

340g/12oz dried tagliatelle

3 tablespoons olive oil

2 cloves garlic, chopped

1 red chilli, deseeded and chopped

finely grated rind of 1 lemon

2 fresh dressed crabs, to give about 310g /11oz crabmeat

200mL/7fl oz single cream

1 tablespoon lemon juice

salt and black pepper

2 tablespoons chopped fresh parsley (garnish)

Method

1. Cook tagliatelle according to the instructions on the packet until tender but still firm to the bite, then drain.

2. Heat olive oil in a large heavy-based frying pan and gently fry garlic, chilli and lemon rind for 3–4 minutes, until softened but not browned. Add crabmeat, cream and lemon juice and simmer for 1–2 minutes to heat through. Season to taste.

3. Transfer tagliatelle to serving bowls. Spoon the crab mixture over the top and sprinkle with parsley and serve immediately

Serves 4.

Spanish Rice with Scampi and Prawns

Ingredients

3 tablespoons olive oil

1 medium onion, finely chopped

2 fresh squid, cleaned and finely chopped

1 large ripe tomato, skinned and chopped

300g/10½ oz short grain rice

3 cups water

pinch saffron threads

salt and ground pepper to taste

8–16 fresh or thawed frozen scampi

500g/1 lb fresh green king prawns

Method

1. In a large, flameproof deep-frying pan, heat oil and gently fry onion and squid for about 5 minutes. Add tomato and cook for 5 more minutes.

2. Add rice and stir to mix well with the squid mixture for 1–2 minutes. Bring water to the boil with saffron, salt and ground pepper, and pour over rice.

3. Add shellfish, leaving scampi either whole or halved and shelling prawns or leaving them whole and unshelled.

4. Simmer over gentle heat until rice is cooked, but don't stir rice at all during the cooking so that shellfish sits on top.

Serves 4

Butterflied Prawns with Garlic, Chilli and Parsley

Ingredients

1kg/2¼ lb green prawns, shelled and deveined with tails intact

2 tablespoons olive oil

1 tablespoon lemon juice

2 cloves garlic, crushed

2 red chillies, seeded and finely chopped

2 tablespoons parsley, chopped

oil

½ cup flour

chopped parsely

lemon wedges

Method

1. Butterfly prawns to ensure even cooking. Set aside.

2. Combine oil, lemon juice, garlic, chilli and parsley in a bowl. Add prawns, mix well, and leave to marinate for 2–3 hours.

3. Heat oil in a large fryingpan, coat prawns with flour, and cook quickly in oil for 2–3 minutes. Drain on absorbent kitchen paper.

4. Serve immediately with lemon wedges and parsley.

Serves 6

Chilli Prawn Pizza

(opposite)

Ingredients

1 frozen pizza base

3 tablespoons tomato paste

2 teaspoons vegetable oil

1 teaspoon ground cumin

3 fresh red chillies, seeded and chopped

2 cloves garlic, crushed

2 tablespoons lemon juice

500g/1 lb uncooked prawns, shelled and deveined

1 red capsicum (pepper), sliced

1 yellow or green capsicum (pepper), sliced

2 tablespoons chopped fresh coriander (cilantro)

2 tablespoons grated Parmesan cheese

freshly ground black pepper

Method

1. Place pizza base on a lightly greased baking tray, spread with tomato paste (purée) and set aside.

2. Heat oil in a frying pan over a medium heat, add cumin, chillies and garlic and cook, stirring, for 1 minute.

3. Stir in lemon juice and prawns and cook for 3 minutes longer or until prawns just change colour and are almost cooked.

4. Top pizza base with red capsicum (pepper), yellow or green capsicum (pepper), then with prawn mixture, coriander, Parmesan cheese and black pepper to taste. Bake for 20 minutes or until base is crisp and golden.

Serves 4

Prawns with Sauce Verte

Ingredients

170mL/6fl oz dry vermouth

2–6 spring onions, chopped

1 sprig fresh parsley

1 bay leaf

salt

freshly ground black pepper

750g/1$^{1}/_{2}$ lb uncooked prawns, shelled and deveined, and tail shells intact

8 small leaves mixed lettuce

chopped fresh parsley and slivered spring onion greens or chives

SAUCE VERTE:

3–4 spinach or young silverbeet leaves, stems removed

170g/6oz mayonnaise

3–4 tablespoons finely chopped fresh parsley

2 tablespoons snipped fresh chives

1 tablespoon finely chopped fresh dill or $^{1}/_{2}$ teaspoon dried

Method

1. Place vermouth, spring onions, parsley sprig and bay leaf in a saucepan, season to taste with salt and black pepper and bring to simmering. Add prawns and simmer for 2–3 minutes or until pink. Drain and cool.

2. To make sauce, steam spinach or silverbeet in a saucepan, covered, over moderate heat for 1 minute. Cool quickly in cold water, drain and pat dry on paper towel. Finely chop. Place mayonnaise in a bowl, add spinach or silverbeet, parsley, chives and dill and mix to combine.

3. To serve, smear a little sauce in a semi-circle on 4 entrée plates. Arrange prawns on sauce, garnish with lettuce leaves and sprinkle with parsley and spring onions or chives.

Serves 4

Fried Mussels

Ingredients

2 eggs, beaten

salt and pepper

1kg/2¼ lb black mussels cleaned, cooked *mariniére* style (see page 237) and removed from shell

2 cups breadcrumbs

1 tablespoon dry mixed aromatic herbs

oil for deep-frying

3 tablespoons tartare sauce

lemon wedges

Method

1. Season eggs with salt and pepper, and put mussels out of their shells in egg mixture.

2. Mix breadcrumbs and dry herbs, and roll mussels in breadcrumbs. Shake to remove excess.

3. Deep-fry coated mussels in oil for a few minutes until golden brown.

4. After cooking drain on absorbent kitchen paper, and serve immediately with tartare sauce, lemon wedges and a green salad.

Serves 4

Spaghetti Marinara

Ingredients

500g/1 lb spaghetti

2 teaspoons vegetable oil

2 teaspoons butter

2 onions, chopped

2 x 400g/14oz cans tomatoes, undrained and mashed

2 tablespoons chopped fresh basil or 1 teaspoon dried basil

$^1/_4$ cup dry white wine

12 mussels, scrubbed and beards removed

12 scallops

12 uncooked prawns, shelled and deveined

125g/4$^1/_2$ oz calamari (squid) rings

Method

1. Cook spaghetti in boiling water in a large saucepan following packet directions. Drain, set aside and keep warm.

2. Heat oil and butter in a frying pan over a medium heat. Add onions and cook, stirring, for 4 minutes or until onions are golden.

3. Stir in tomatoes, basil and wine, bring to simmering point and simmer for 8 minutes. Add mussels, scallops and prawns and cook for 2 minutes longer.

4. Add calamari and cook for 1 minute or until shellfish is cooked. Spoon shellfish mixture over hot spaghetti and serve immediately.

Serves 4

Tuna Nicoise

Ingredients

170g/6oz fine green beans, cut in $7^1/_2$cm /3in lengths

4 tablespoons olive oil

4 tuna steaks, about 170g/6oz each and $2^1/_2$cm/1in thick

salt and black pepper

1 red capsicum (pepper), deseeded and diced

12 cherry tomatoes, halved

16 black olives, pitted

1 tablespoon balsamic vinegar

fresh flat-leaf parsley or coriander

Method

1. Cook beans in boiling salted water for 3–5 minutes, until tender but still firm to the bite. Drain, refresh under cold water and set aside. Place 2 tablespoons of oil in a shallow bowl, add tuna and turn to coat, then season lightly.

2. Heat a large heavy-based frying pan over a high heat, then add tuna and cook for 1 minute on each side. Reduce the heat and cook for a further 1–2 minutes on each side, until steaks have slightly browned. Set aside.

3. Heat remaining oil in the fryingpan and fry the red capsicum (pepper) for 1 minute or until softened. Add the beans, tomatoes and olives and stir-fry for 1 minute to warm through. Remove from the heat and pour in vinegar. Serve tuna topped with the capsicum (pepper) mixture and scatter over parsley or coriander.

Serves 4

Braised Prawns with Chinese Greens

Ingredients

750g/1$^{2}/_{3}$ lb green prawns, shelled and deveined

1 tablespoon Chinese wine or dry sherry

1 teaspoon cornflour

1 teaspoon soy sauce

12 snow peas (mangetout)

1 bunch Chinese flowering cabbage

5 tablespoons oil

SEASONING:

$^{1}/_{2}$ teaspoon salt

$^{1}/_{2}$ teaspoon sugar

2 teaspoon soy sauce

1 teaspoon sesame oil

Method

1. Put prawns into a bowl with wine or sherry, cornflour and soy sauce. Mix well, cover and chill for at least 30 minutes.

2. Heat 4 tablespoons of oil in a wok and cook prawns until their colour changes. Remove. Add rest of oil to the wok and cook vegetables for 2 minutes.

3. Return prawns to the wok and add seasoning. Toss until heated through, and serve immediately.

Serves 4

Scallops with Zucchini in Apple Butter

(opposite)

Ingredients

2 zucchini (courgettes), cut into 2$^1/_2$cm/1in thick slices

8 large scallops with their corals

1 tablespoon olive oil

salt and black pepper

85mL/3fl oz apple juice

30g/1oz butter

fresh flat-leaf parsley

Method

1. Turn zucchini (courgette) and scallops gently in oil and season.

2. Heat a large heavy-based frying pan until hot, add zucchini (courgette) and cook for 2 minutes on one side. Turn over and add scallops to the pan. Cook for 1 minute, then turn over the scallops. Cook both scallops and zucchini (courgettes) for a further minute, until scallops are golden and zucchini (courgette) slices are browned.

3. Remove scallops and zucchini (courgette) from the frying pan and keep warm. Pour apple juice into the frying pan, add butter and cook until reduced to a syrupy sauce. Spoon sauce over scallops and zucchini (courgette) and garnish with parsley.

Serves 4

Scallops Santiago Style

Ingredients

2 tablespoons olive oil

4 tablespoons finely chopped onion

2 cloves garlic, minced

500g/1 lb bay scallops (or sea scallops cut in halves)

2 tablespoons chopped parsley

$^1/_2$ teaspoon thyme

1 dried red chilli pepper, seeds removed and crumbled

salt freshly ground pepper

2 cups sliced mushrooms

2 tablespoons brandy, preferably Spanish brandy, or Cognac

$^3/_4$ cup dry white wine

$^1/_2$ cup tomato sauce, preferably home-made

bread crumbs

butter

Method

1. Heat olive oil in a frying pan and saute onion and garlic until onion is wilted. Add the scallops and cook over high heat for 2 minutes, stirring. (Scallops should not give off liquid; if they do, remove and evaporate the liquid.) Lower the heat and sprinkle in parsley, thyme, chilli pepper, salt and pepper. Add mushrooms and cook for 5 minutes then pour in brandy and flame. Remove scallops and mushrooms, and arrange them in scallop shells or individual casseroles. Add wine and tomato sauce to the frying pan and bring to the boil. Season if necessary and, simmer for 10 minutes, uncovered.

2. Pour sauce over scallops. Sprinkle with breadcrumbs and dot with butter. Bake at 230°C/450°F for about 10 minutes. Serve immediately with a green salad and a medium dry white wine.

Serves 4-6

Snapper Fillets with White Wine and Parsley

Ingredients

½ cup flour

1 teaspoon coarsly ground pepper

¼ teaspoon sea salt

4 snapper fillets, each 225g/8oz

2 tablespoons olive oil

55g/2oz butter

2 cloves garlic, crushed

½ cup white wine

2 tablespoons parsley, finely chopped

Method

1. Combine flour, pepper and salt in a dish, and coat fish fillets evenly with flour, shaking off excess.

2. Heat olive oil in a pan, add fish, and cook over a medium heat for 5–6 minutes on each side, depending on thickness of fish. Set fish aside on a plate, and keep warm.

3. Wipe out the frying pan, then melt butter, add garlic, and cook for 2 minutes. Add white wine and simmer, until sauce reduces. Just before serving, add chopped parsley to sauce and serve with fish.

Serves 4

Scampi with basil butter

Ingredients

8 uncooked scampi or yabbies, heads removed

BASIL BUTTER:

85g/3oz butter, melted

2 tablespoons chopped fresh basil

1 clove garlic, crushed

2 teaspoons honey

Method

1. Cut scampi or yabbies in half lengthwise.

2. To make basil butter, place butter, basil, garlic and honey in a small bowl and whisk to combine.

3. Brush cut side of each scampi or yabby half with basil butter and cook under a preheated hot grill for 2 minutes or until they change colour and are tender. Drizzle with any remaining basil butter and serve immediately.

Serves 8

light meals

Black Forest Mussels with Mushrooms and Brandy

Ingredients

30g/1oz butter

$^1/_2$ onion, finely chopped

1 clove garlic, chopped

145g/5oz finely sliced black forest mushrooms or field mushrooms

1kg/$2^1/_4$ lb black mussels, cleaned and beards removed

100mL/$3^1/_2$ fl oz white wine

salt and pepper to taste

2 tablespoons double cream

30mL/1fl oz brandy

fresh parsley, chopped

Method

1. Put butter, onion, garlic and mushrooms in a saucepan, and cook on a high heat for 5 minutes. Add mussels, white wine and seasoning. Cook mussels until all have opened, stirring frequently. Discard any that don't open.

2. Add cream and stir for 30 seconds. Then add brandy and cook for 1 more minute.

3. Serve immediately with a sprinkle of chopped parsley on top.

Serves 3 – 4

Penne with Prawns and Saffron Sauce

Ingredients

500g/1 lb penne

500g/1 lb cooked prawns, shelled and deveined

115g/4oz snow peas (mangetout), blanched

SAFFRON SAUCE:

30g/1oz butter

1 tablespoon flour

1 cup reduced-fat milk

1/2 teaspoon saffron threads or pinch saffron powder

1 tablespoon chopped fresh sage or 1/2 teaspoon dried sage

Method

1. Cook penne in boiling water in a large saucepan following packet directions. Drain, set aside and keep warm.

2. To make sauce, melt butter in a small saucepan over a medium heat, stir in flour and cook for 1 minute. Remove the saucepan from the heat and whisk in milk, saffron and sage. Return the saucepan to heat and cook, stirring, for 3–4 minutes or until sauce boils and thickens.

3. Add prawns and snow peas (mangetout) to hot penne and toss to combine. Top with sauce and serve immediately.

Serves 4

Prawns with Spinach

Ingredients

100mL/3½ fl oz olive oil

1 onion, diced

1 red capsicum (pepper), seeded and diced

1 clove garlic, crushed

2 tomatoes, peeled and diced

1½ bunches spinach, washed and roughly chopped

2 tablespoons dry white wine

juice of 1 lemon

salt and freshly ground black pepper

500g/1 lb green prawns, shelled and deveined with tails left on

lemon wedges

Method

1. Heat 2 tablespoons of olive oil in a saucepan and add onion and brown. Add red capsicum (bell pepper), garlic and tomatoes, and cook for 7 minutes. Add spinach, white wine, lemon juice and seasoning.

2. Cover and simmer gently for 8–10 minutes or until the spinach is tender. Take off the heat, stir and keep warm.

3. Add remaining olive oil to a large frying pan. Once hot, add prawns and sauté, stirring constantly, for 3 minutes, or until just cooked.

4. Spoon prawns into spinach, fold to combine, and spoon onto a warm serving platter. Serve with lemon wedges.

Serves 4

Chargrilled Scallops with Pinapple Salsa

Ingredients

30 scallops

chilli or lime oil

crisp tortilla chips

PINEAPPLE SALSA:

115g/4oz chopped pineapple

$^1/_4$ red capsicum (pepper), finely chopped

2 medium green chillies, chopped

1 tablespoon fresh coriander leaves

1 tablespoon fresh mint leaves

1 tablespoon lime juice

Method

1. To make salsa, place pineapple, red capsicum (pepper), chillies, coriander, mint and lime juice in a bowl, toss to combine, then stand for 20 minutes.

2. Brush scallops with oil and cook on a preheated hot chargrill or barbecue plate for 30 seconds on each side or until they just change colour. Serve immediately with salsa and tortilla chips.

Serves 4

Crispy Trout with Almonds and Ginger Sauce

Ingredients

salt and black pepper

4 rainbow trout, cleaned and boned

2 tablespoons plain flour

2 tablespoons vegetable oil

85g/3oz fresh root ginger, grated

30g/1oz butter

85g/3oz flaked almonds

2 tablespoons currants

Method

1. Season fish and dust with flour. Heat oil in a large non stick frying pan over a medium-high heat, add fish and cook for 5 minutes on each side or until crisp, golden and cooked through. Remove fish from the frying pan and keep warm.

2. Squeeze grated ginger over a small bowl to extract the juice – you should have 4–6 teaspoons.

3. Add butter and almonds to the frying pan, and cook gently for 2 minutes or until almonds are golden. Add currants and ginger juice, heat through for a few seconds, then spoon over fish and serve immediately.

Serves 4

Mussels Mariniéres

Ingredients

1kg/2 1/4 lb mussels, cleaned

1 small onion, sliced

1 stalk celery, sliced

1 clove garlic, chopped

55mL/2fl oz water or white wine

pepper

1 tablespoon butter

1 tablespoon parsley, chopped

Method

1. Put mussels in a casserole with onion, celery, garlic and water or white wine.

2. Cook until mussels have opened, stirring frequently to make sure mussels are cooked evenly.

3. Season with pepper, then add butter and parsley to mussels and stir. Serve immediately with fresh crusty bread

Serves 4

Swordfish Steaks with Tomato Salsa

Ingredients

55g/2oz basil pesto

20mL/2/3 fl oz olive oil

4 swordfish steaks

extra oil, for the chargrill

TOMATO SALSA:

2 Roma tomatoes, finely chopped

1 small red onion, finely chopped

1 teaspoon coarse black pepper

2 tablespoons basil, chopped

40mL/1 1/3 fl oz extra virgin olive oil

20mL/2/3 fl oz lemon juice

Method

1. Combine basil pesto and olive oil. Brush fish with pesto and set aside.

2. Preheat the chargrill, oil lightly and cook fish for 2–3 minutes each side.

3. To make salsa, combine all salsa ingredients in a small bowl, and mix well.

4. Serve fish with salsa over the top.

Serves 4

Linguine with Prawns and Scallops in a Roasted Tomato Sauce

Ingredients

400g/14oz linguine

1kg/2$^{1}/_{4}$ lb tomatoes

a little olive oil salt and pepper

85mL/3fl oz olive oil

200g/7oz scallops

200g/7oz green prawns, peeled

145g/5oz calamari, cut into rings

200g/7oz firm white fish pieces

3 cloves garlic, crushed

2 brown onions, diced

1 tablespoon tomato paste (optional)

85mL/3fl oz water

$^{1}/_{2}$ bunch parsley, chopped

Parmesan cheese

Method

1. Cook linguine in salted boiling water until *al dente* and set aside.

2. To roast tomatoes, preheat the oven to 180°C/350°F. Cut tomatoes in half and place on a baking tray. Drizzle with olive oil, sprinkle with salt and pepper, and roast in the oven for 20–25 minutes.

3. Place tomatoes in a food processor and process for a few seconds, but do not over process. (The mixture should still have texture.)

4. Heat half the oil in a frying pan, and sauté scallops and prawns for 2 minutes or until just cooked. Remove from the pan and add calamari and cook for 2 minutes, before removing from the pan. Adding a little more oil if needed, sauté fish for a few minutes until just cooked, and remove from the pan.

5. Heat remaining oil, and sauté garlic and onions for a few minutes until cooked. Add tomato mixture, tomato paste and water, and simmer for 10 minutes. Carefully add seafood to the sauce, season with salt and pepper, and mix through chopped parsley. Serve with linguine and Parmesan cheese.

Serves 4

Salmon Cutlets with Dill Hollandaise Sauce

Ingredients

40mL/1$^{1}/_{3}$ fl oz extra virgin olive oil

1 tablespoon lemon juice

$^{1}/_{4}$ teaspoon coarse black pepper

4 x 200g/7oz salmon cutlets

a little extra oil

DILL HOLLANDAISE SAUCE:

85mL/3fl oz white wine vinegar

freshly ground pepper

55mL/2fl oz water

4 egg yolks

200g/7oz unsalted butter, melted

40mL/1$^{1}/_{3}$ fl oz lemon juice

3 tablespoons fresh dill, chopped

extra freshly ground pepper and salt

Method

1. Combine oil, lemon juice and pepper in a large ceramic dish. Add salmon cutlets and eave to marinate for 3–4 hours.

2. To make the dill hollandaise sauce, in a small saucepan add vinegar, pepper and water. Bring to the boil, then reduce, until 1 tablespoon of the liquid is left. Place egg yolks and vinegar mixture in a food processor, and process for 1 minute. With the motor still running, gradually add hot melted butter, and process until thick. Add lemon juice, dill, and salt and pepper to taste, and keep warm.

3. To cook salmon cutlets, lightly oil and heat a chargrill pan, or preheat a grill. Cook salmon cutlets for 2–3 minutes on each side or until done to your liking.

4. Serve salmon immediately with dill hollandaise sauce drizzled over and potato wedges.

Serves 4

Spicy Prawns with Sun-Dried Tomatoes

Ingredients

3 tablespoons olive oil

1kg/2 1/4 lb green king prawns, peeled and deveined with tails intact

1 tablespoon tomato paste

2 teaspoons brown sugar

2 cloves garlic, crushed

1 tablespoon chilli sauce

1 tablespoon coriander, chopped

3/4 cup sun-dried tomatoes, drained

1 tablespoon fresh lime juice

snow pea sprouts

Method

1. Heat oil in a frying pan over a moderate heat. Add prawns and cook for 1 minute on each side. Remove prawns with a slotted spoon and set aside.

2. Add tomato paste, sugar, garlic, chilli sauce and coriander to the frying pan and cook for 1 minute.

3. Return prawns to the frying pan and add sun-dried tomatoes. Toss prawns in sauce and sprinkle with lime juice. Place prawns onto a serving plate, and serve with snow pea sprouts.

Serves 4

Prawn Tacos

(opposite)

Ingredients

8 flour tortillas, warmed

145g/5oz feta cheese, crumbled

SEAFOOD FILLING:

2 teaspoons vegetable oil

1 onion, chopped

2 tomatoes, chopped

370g/13oz white fish, cubed

255g/9 oz medium uncooked prawns, shelled and deveined

12 scallops

3 medium-sized fresh green chillies, chopped

2 tablespoons chopped fresh oregano

1 teaspoon finely grated lemon rind

Method

1. To make filling, heat oil in a frying pan over a high heat, add onion and cook for 4 minutes or until golden. Add tomatoes and cook for 5 minutes. Add fish, prawns, scallops, chillies, oregano and lemon rind and cook, tossing, for 3–4 minutes or until seafood is cooked.

2. To serve, spoon filling down the centre of each tortilla and scatter with feta cheese. Fold tortilla to enclose filling and serve immediately.

Serves 4

Peppered Prawns

Ingredients

750g/1$^{2}/_{3}$ lb green king prawns

1 small chicken stock cube

2 teaspoons cornflour

$^{1}/_{2}$ cup water

2 tablespoons soy sauce

1 tablespoon dry sherry

2 tablespoons tomato sauce

1 clove garlic, crushed

2 teaspoons cracked black peppercorns

1 tablespoon honey

2 tablespoons oil

500g/1 lb broccoli, cut into florets

400g/14oz canned baby corn, drained

1 onion, sliced

1 stalk celery, thinly sliced

1 red capsicum (pepper), thinly sliced

cornflour, extra

1 tablespoon water, extra

Method

1. Peel and devein prawns, leaving tails intact. Mix together chicken stock cube, cornflour and water, and set aside.

2. Combine soy sauce, sherry, tomato sauce, garlic, peppercorns and honey in a large dish. Add prawns, cover, and refrigerate for several hours.

3. Heat oil in a wok or large frying pan. Add vegetables, and stir-fry for about 2 minutes.

4. Add prawns and marinade to the wok, and cook, stirring, over high heat until prawns change colour and are cooked.

5. Stir in extra cornflour, combinec with extra water, and cook, stirring, unti smooth.

Serves 4 – 6

Spaghettini with Baby Clams, Chilli and Garlic

(opposite)

Ingredients

680g/$1\frac{1}{2}$ lb canned baby clams, or fresh if available

400g/14oz spaghettini

85mL/3fl oz olive oil

4 cloves garlic, sliced

4 red chillies, finely chopped

2 cups tomato, finely diced

$\frac{1}{3}$ cup parsley, chopped

juice of 2 lemons

salt and freshly ground black pepper

Method

1. If using fresh clams, wash under running water, scraping the shells with a sharp knife or scourer. Put them in a large saucepan with a little water over a gentle heat until they open. Discard any that do not open.

2. Cook spaghettini in boiling water with a little oil until *al dente*. Run under cold water until cold and set aside.

3. Heat half the oil and cook garlic on a low heat until beginning to change colour. Add chilli and tomato, and cook for a few minutes.

3. Add clams, parsley, lemon juice, remaining oil, spaghettini and a little of water used to cook fresh clams, if using, and heat through for a further 5 minutes. Season with salt and black ground pepper.

1. If using fresh clams, wash under running water, scraping the shells with a sharp knife or scourer. Put them in a large pan with a little water over a gentle heat until they open. Discard any that do not open.

Serves 4-6

Linguine with Mussels and Ham

Ingredients:

200mL/7fl oz dry white wine

1kg/$2\frac{1}{4}$ lb black mussels cleaned and beards removed

3 tablespoons chopped fresh parsley

3 tablespoons snipped fresh chives

30g/1oz butter

85g/3oz Parma ham, cut into ribbons

$1\frac{1}{2}$ bunches spinach, washed and roughly chopped

salt and black pepper

750g/$1\frac{2}{3}$ lb fresh linguine

Method

1. Bring white wine to the boil in a large saucepan. Tip in mussels and their juices and sprinkle over 2 tablespoons each of the parsley and chives. Cover and cook for 3 minutes or until mussels open up. Strain over a large bowl, reserving cooking liquid, then leave for a few minutes until cool enough to handle. Shell most of mussels, discarding any that are unopened or broken and reserving a few on the half shell to garnish.

2. Melt half the butter in a frying pan over a high heat. Tip in ham, stir for 1 minute, then add spinach and cook for 2–3 minutes, still stirring. Add drained mussels to the pan with a little of their cooking liquid, then reduce the heat and heat through. Meanwhile, bring a large saucepan of water to the boil. Season with salt and cook linguine according to the packet instructions.

3. Drain linguine and transfer to a large serving dish. Top with the rest of butter, reserved mussel liquid and half remaining herbs. Toss, then tip over mussel and ham mixture and toss again. Scatter over the rest of herbs, season and garnish with mussels on the half shell.

Serves 4

Fish and Chips with Tartare Sauce

Ingredients

85g/3oz plain flour

$^{1}/_{2}$ teaspoon salt

1 tablespoon vegetable oil

115mL/4fl oz cold water

4 large potatoes, cut into chunky chips

oil for deep-frying

1 large egg white

4 pieces white-fleshed fish fillets, about 170g/6oz each

salt flakes to serve

TARTARE SAUCE:

$^{3}/_{5}$ cup mayonnaise

1 tablespoon capers, drained and chopped

1 tablespoon chopped gherkin

1 tablespoon chopped fresh parsley

1 teaspoon finely chopped shallot

Method

1. To make sauce, combine mayonnaise, capers, gherkin, parsley and shallot in a bowl. Cover and place in the refrigerator.

2. Mix flour, salt and oil with 115mL/4fl oz of cold water to make a batter.

3. Cover chips with cold water, then drain and dry on kitchen towels. Heat oil in a large heavy-based saucepan. Test that oil is ready by adding a potato chip – it should sizzle immediately. Cook chips in 3 or 4 batches for 5–7 minutes each, until golden and cooked. Drain on kitchen towels and keep warm. Whisk egg white until stiff (this is easiest with an electric whisk) and fold into the batter.

4. Reduce the heat a little and drop a teaspoon of batter into the oil – it should bubble and firm up straight away. Dip pieces of fish into batter, coating well, then cook for 5–7 minutes, until crisp and golden, then drain on kitchen towels. Serve sprinkled with salt, with chips and tartare sauce.

Serves 4

Cod Fillet with Cheddar and Tomato Topping

Ingredients

butter for greasing

145g/5oz mature cheddar cheese, grated

4 tsp wholegrain mustard

4 tbsp crème fraîche

4 pieces thick blue-eye cod, each about 170g/6oz

salt and black pepper

3 tomatoes, sliced

Method

1. Preheat the oven to 200°C/400°F and grease 4 individual gratin dishes.

2. Mix together Cheddar, mustard and crème fraîche. Place a piece of fish in each dish and season lightly. Top with tomato slices, then spoon over the cheese mixture.

3. Cook at the top of the oven for 25 minutes, until cheese has melted and is turning golden and fish is firm and cooked through.

Serves 4

Pan-Fried Squid with Lemon

Ingredients

680g/1½ lb squid tubes

½ cup fine semolina

1 teaspoon salt

1 teaspoon ground pepper

1 cup olive oil, for frying

1 lemon, cut into wedges

Method

1. Cut each tube of squid along 1 side. With a sharp knife score inside skin diagonally in both directions. Cut squid into rectangles, each 2 x 4cm/1x1½in.

2. In a bowl, combine semolina, salt and pepper.

3. Heat oil in a large frying pan or wok. Dip squid into semolina, and when oil is hot, cook a few pieces at a time until lightly brown and crisp. Drain on absorbent kitchen paper and serve with lemon wedges.

Serves 4

Baked Fish

Ingredients

$1^1/_2$ kg/$3^1/_3$ lb whole snapper

salt and pepper

juice of 1 lemon

$^1/_2$ cup olive oil

1 large onion, sliced

3 cloves garlic, thinly sliced

$^1/_2$ cup celery, chopped

425g/15oz canned tomato pieces, peeled

$^1/_2$ cup dry white wine (optional)

$^1/_2$ teaspoon sugar

1 teaspoon oregano

Method

1. Prepare fish, leaving head and tail on. Make diagonal cuts on surface, sprinkle with a little salt and pepper and lemon juice. Set aside for 20 minutes.

2. Heat half the oil in a frying pan, and sauté onion, garlic and celery for 3 minutes. Add tomatoes, wine if using, sugar and oregano, and season with salt and pepper. Sauté a further 2 minutes.

3. Spread mixture into an oiled baking dish and place fish on top. Drizzle remaining oil over fish. Bake in a pre-heated oven 180°C/350°F for 30–40 minutes, depending on size. Baste fish during cooking.

4. Remove fish to a serving platter, spoon sauce around fish, and serve with vegetables or a salad.

Serves 4

glossary

acidulated water: water with added acid, such as lemon juice or vinegar, which prevents discoloration of ingredients, particularly fruit or vegetables. The proportion of acid to water is 1 teaspoon per 300ml.

al dente: Italian cooking term for ingredients that are cooked until tender but still firm to the bite; usually applied to pasta.

americaine: method of serving seafood - usually lobster and monkfish - in a sauce flavoured with olive oil, aromatic herbs, tomatoes, white wine, fish stock, brandy and tarragon.

anglaise: cooking style for simple cooked dishes such as boiled vegetables. Assiette anglaise is a plate of cold cooked meats.

antipasto: Italian for "before the meal", it denotes an assortment of cold meats, vegetables and cheeses, often marinated, served as an hors d'oeuvre. A typical antipasto might include salami, prosciutto, marinated artichoke hearts, anchovy fillets, olives, tuna fish and Provolone cheese.

au gratin: food sprinkled with breadcrumbs, often covered with cheese sauce and browned until a crisp coating forms.

balsamic vinegar: a mild, extremely fragrant wine-based vinegar made in northern Italy. Traditionally, the vinegar is aged for at least seven years in a series of casks made of various woods.

baste: to moisten food while it is cooking by spooning or brushing on liquid or fat.

baine marie: a saucepan standing in a large pan which is filled with boiling water to keep liquids at simmering point. A double boiler will do the same job.

beat: to stir thoroughly and vigorously.

beurre manie: equal quantities of butter and flour kneaded together and added a little at a time to thicken a stew or casserole.

bird: see paupiette.

blanc: a cooking liquid made by adding flour and lemon juice to water in order to keep certain vegetables from discolouring as they cook.

blanch: to plunge into boiling water and then in some cases, into cold water. Fruits and nuts are blanched to remove skin easily.

blanquette: a white stew of lamb, veal or chicken, bound with egg yolks and cream and accompanied by onion and mushrooms.

blend: to mix thoroughly.

bonne femme: dishes cooked in the traditional French "housewife" style. Chicken and pork bonne femme are garnished with bacon, potatoes and baby onion; fish bonne femme with mushrooms in a white wine sauce.

bouguet garni: a bunch of herbs, usually consisting of sprigs of parsley, thyme, marjoram, rosemary, a bay leaf, peppercorns and cloves, tied in muslin and used to flavour stews and casseroles.

braise: to cook whole or large pieces of poultry, game, fish, meat or vegetables in a small amount of wine, stock or other liquid in a closed pot. Often the main ingredient is first browned in fat and then cooked in a low oven or very slowly on top of the stove. Braising suits tough meats and older birds and produces a mellow, rich sauce.

broil: The American term for grilling food.

brown: cook in a small amount of fat until brown.

burghul (also bulgur): a type of cracked wheat, where the kernels are steamed and dried before being crushed.

buttered: to spread with softened or melted butter.

butterfly: to slit a piece of food in half horizontally, cutting it almost through so that when opened it resembles butterfly wings. Chops, large prawns and thick fish fillets are often butterflied so that they cook more quickly.

buttermilk: a tangy, low-fat cultured milk product whose slight acidity makes it an ideal marinade base for poultry.

calzone: a semicircular pocket of pizza dough, stuffed with meat or vegetables, sealed and baked.

caramelise: to melt sugar until it is a golden brown syrup.

champignons: small mushrooms, usually canned.

chasseur: (hunter) a French cooking style in which meat and chicken dishes are cooked with mushrooms, shallots, white wine, and often tomato.

clarify: to melt butter and drain the oil off the sediment.

coat: to cover with a thin layer of flour, sugar, nuts, crumbs, poppy or sesame seeds, cinnamon sugar or a few of the ground spices.

concasser: to chop coarsely, usually tomatoes.

confit: from the French verb confire, meaning to preserve. Food that is made into a preserve by cooking very slowly and thoroughly until tender. In the case of meat, such as duck or goose, it is cooked in its own fat, and covered with it so that it does not come into contact with the air. Vegetables such as onions are good inconfit.

consomme: a clear soup usually made from beef.

coulis: a thin puree, usually of fresh or cooked fruit or vegetables, which is soft enough to pour (couler means to run). A coulis may be rough-textured or very smooth.

court bouillon: the liquid in which fish, poultry or meat is cooked. It usually consists of water with bay leaf, onion, carrots and salt and freshly ground black pepper to taste. Other additives can include wine, vinegar, stock, garlic or spring onions (scallions).

couscous: cereal processed from semolina into pellets, traditionally steamed and served with meat and vegetables in the classic North African stew of the same name.

cruciferous vegetables: certain members of the mustard, cabbage and turnip families with cross-shaped flowers and strong aromas and flavours.

cream: to make soft, smooth and creamy by rubbing with back of spoon or by beating with mixer. Usually applied to fat and sugar.

croutons: small toasted or fried cubes of bread.

crudites: raw vegetables, whether cut in slices or sticks to nibble plain or with a dipping sauce, or shredded and tossed as salad with a simple dressing.

cube: to cut into small pieces with 6 equal sides.

curdle: to cause milk or sauce to separate into solid and liquid. Example, overcooked egg mixtures.

daikon radish (also called mooli): a long white Japanese radish. dark sesame oil (also called Oriental sesame oil): dark polyunsaturated oil with a low burning point, used for seasoning. Do not replace with lighter sesame oil.

deglaze: to dissolve congealed cooking juices or glaze on the bottom of a pan by adding a liquid, then scraping and stirring vigorously whilst bringing the liquid to the boil. Juices may be used to make gravy or to add to sauce.

degrease: to skim grease from the surface of liquid. If possible the liquid should be chilled so the fat solidifies. If not, skim off most of the fat with a large metal spoon, then trail strips of paper towel on the surface of the liquid to remove any remaining globules.

devilled: a dish or sauce that is highly seasoned with a hot ingredient such as mustard, Worcestershire sauce or cayenne pepper.

dice: to cut into small cubes.

dietary fibre: a plant-cell material that is undigested or only partially digested in the human body, but which promotes healthy digestion of other food matter.

dissolve: mix a dry ingredient with liquid until absorbed.

dredge: to coat with a dry ingredient, as flour or sugar.

drizzle: to pour in a fine thread-like stream over a surface.

dust: to sprinkle or coat lightly with flour or icing sugar.

Dutch oven: a heavy casserole with a lid usually made from cast iron or pottery.

emulsion: a mixture of two liquids that are not mutually soluble - for example, oil and water.

entree: in Europe, the "entry" or hors d'oeuvre; in North America entree means the main course.

fillet: special cut of beef, lamb, pork or veal; breast of poultry and game; fish cut of the bone lengthways.

flake: to break into small pieces with a fork.

flame: to ignite warmed alcohol over food.

fold in: a gentle, careful combining of a light or delicate mixture with a heavier mixture using a metal spoon.

fricassee: a dish in which poultry, fish or vegetables are bound together with a white or veloute sauce. In Britain and the United States, the name applies to an old-fashioned dish of chicken in a creamy sauce.

galette: sweet or savoury mixture shaped as a flat round.

garnish: to decorate food, usually with something edible.

gastrique: caramelized sugar deglazed with vinegar and used in fruit-flavoured savoury sauces, in such dishes as duck with orange.

glaze: a thin coating of beaten egg, syrup or aspic which is brushed over pastry, fruits or cooked meats.

gluten: a protein in flour that is developed when dough is kneaded, making it elastic.

gratin: a dish cooked in the oven or under the grill so that it develops a brown crust. Breadcrumbs or cheese may be sprinkled on top first. Shallow gratin dishes ensure a maximum area of crust.

grease: to rub or brush lightly with oil or fat.

infuse: to immerse herbs, spices or other flavourings in hot liquid to flavour it. Infusion takes from two to five minutes depending on the flavouring. The liquid should be very hot but not boiling.

jardiniere: a garnish of garden vegetables, typically carrots, pickling onions, French beans and turnips.

joint: to cut poultry, game or small animals into serving pieces by dividing at the joint.

julienne: to cut food into match-like strips.

knead: to work dough using heel of hand with a pressing motion, while stretching and folding the dough.

lights: lungs of an animal, used in various meat preparations such as pates and faggots.

line: to cover the inside of a container with paper, to protect or aid in removing mixture.

macerate: to soak food in liquid to soften.

marinade: a seasoned liquid, usually an oil and acid mixture, in which meats or other foods are soaked to soften and give more flavour.

marinara: Italian "sailor's style" cooking that does not apply to any particular combination of ingredients. Marinara tomato sauce for pasta is most familiar.

marinate: to let food stand in a marinade to season and tenderize.

mask: to cover cooked food with sauce.

melt: to heat until liquified.

mince: to grind into very small pieces.

mix: to combine ingredients by stirring.

monounsaturated fats: one of three types of fats found in foods. Are believed not to raise the level of cholesterol in the blood.

nicoise: a garnish of tomatoes, garlic and black olives; a salad with anchovy, tuna and French beans is typical.

non-reactive pan: a cooking pan whose surface does not chemically react with food. Materials used include stainless steel, enamel, glass and some alloys.

noisette: small "nut" of lamb cut from boned loin or rack that is rolled, tied and cut in neat slices. Noisette also means flavoured with hazelnuts, or butter cooked to a nut brown colour.

normande: a cooking style for fish, with a garnish of shrimp, mussels and mushrooms in a white wine cream sauce; for poultry and meat, a sauce with cream, Calvados and apple.

olive oil: various grades of oil extract from olives. Extra virgin olive oil has a full, fruity flavour and the lowest acidity. Virgin olive oil is slightly higher in acidity and lighter in flavour. Pure olive oil is a processed blend of olive oils and has the highest acidity and lightest taste.

panade: a mixture for binding stuffings and dumplings, notably quenelles, often of choux pastry or simply breadcrumbs. A panade may also be made of frangipane, pureed potatoes or rice.

papillote: to cook food in oiled or buttered greasepoof paper or aluminium foil. Also a decorative frill to cover bone ends of chops and poultry drumsticks.

parboil: to boil or simmer until part cooked (i.e. cooked further than when blanching).

pare: to cut away outside covering.

pate: a paste of meat or seafood used as a spread for toast or crackers.

paupiette: a thin slice of meat, poultry or fish spread with a savoury stuffing and rolled. In the United States this is also called "bird" and in Britain an "olive".

peel: to strip away outside covering.

plump: to soak in liquid or moisten thoroughly until full and round.

poach: to simmer gently in enough hot liquid to cover, using care to retain shape of food.

polyunsaturated fat: one of the three types of fats found in food. These exist in large quantities in such vegetable oils as safflower, sunflower, corn and soya bean. These fats lower the level of cholesterol in the blood.

puree: a smooth paste, usually of vegetables or fruits, made by putting foods through a sieve, food mill or liquefying in a blender or food processor.

ragout: traditionally a well-seasoned, rich stew containing meat, vegetables and wine. Nowadays, a term applied to any stewed mixture.

ramekins: small oval or round individual baking dishes.reconstitute: to put moisture back into dehydrated foods by soaking in liquid.

reduce: to cook over a very high heat, uncovered, until the liquid is reduced by evaporation.

refresh: to cool hot food quickly, either under running water or by plunging it into iced water, to stop it cooking. Particularly for vegetables and occasionally for shellfish.

rice vinegar: mild, fragrant vinegar that is less sweet than cider vinegar and not as harsh as distilled malt vinegar. Japanese rice vinegar is milder than the Chinese variety.

roulade: a piece of meat, usually pork or veal, that is spread with stuffing, rolled and often braised or poached. A roulade may also be a sweet or savoury mixture that is baked in a Swiss roll tin or paper case, filled with a contrasting filling, and rolled.

rubbing-in: a method of incorporating fat into flour, by use of fingertips only. Also incorporates air into mixture.

safflower oil: the vegetable oil that contains the highest proportion of polyunsaturated fats.

salsa: a juice derived from the main ingredient being cooked or a sauce added to a dish to enhance its flavour. In Italy the term is often used for pasta sauces; in Mexico the name usually applies to uncooked sauces served as an accompaniment, especially to corn chips.

saturated fats: one of the three types of fats found in foods. These exist in large quantities in animal products, coconut and palm oils; they raise the level of cholesterol in the blood. As high cholesterol levels may cause heart disease, saturated fat consumption is recommended to be less than 15% of kilojoules provided by the daily diet.

sauté: to cook or brown in small amount of hot fat.

score: to mark food with cuts, notches of lines to prevent curling or to make food more attractive.

scald: to bring just to boiling point, usually for milk. Also to rinse with boiling water.

sear: to brown surface quickly over high heat in hot dish.

seasoned flour: flour with salt and pepper added.

sift: to shake a dry, powdered substance through a sieve or sifter to remove any lumps and give lightness.

simmer: to cook food gently in liquid that bubbles steadily just below boiling point so that the food cooks in even heat without breaking up.

singe: to quickly flame poultry to remove all traces of feathers after plucking.

skim: to remove a surface layer (often of impurities and scum) from a liquid with a metal spoon or small ladle.

slivered: sliced in long, thin pieces, usually refers to nuts, especially almonds.

soften: re gelatine - sprinkle over cold water and allow to gel (soften) then dissolve and liquefy.

souse: to cover food, particularly fish, in wine vinegar and spices and cook slowly; the food is cooled in the same liquid. Sousing gives food a pickled flavour.

steep: to soak in warm or cold liquid in order to soften food and draw out strong flavours or impurities.

stir-fry: to cook thin slices of meat and vegetable over a high heat in a small amount of oil, stirring constantly to even cooking in a short time. Traditionally cooked in a wok, however a heavy based frying pan may be used.

stock: a liquid containing flavours, extracts and nutrients of bones, meat, fish or vegetables.

stud: to adorn with; for example, baked ham studded with whole cloves.

sweat: to cook vegetables over heat until on y juices run.

sugo: an Italian sauce made from the liquid or juice extracted from fruit or meat during cooking.

sweat: to cook sliced or chopped food, usually vegetables, in a little fat and no liquid over very low heat. Foil is pressed on top so that the food steams in its own juices, usually before being added to other dishes.

timbale: a creamy mixture of vegetables or meat baked in a mould. French for "kettledrum"; also denotes a drum-shaped baking dish.

thicken: to make a thin, smooth paste by mixing together arrowroot, cornflour or flour with an equal amount of cold water; stir into hot liquid, cook, stirring until thickened.

toss: to gently mix ingredients with two forks or fork spoon.

total fat: the individual daily intake of all three fats previously described in this glossary. Nutritionists recommend that fats provide no more than 35% of the energy in the diet.

vine leaves: tender, lightly flavoured leaves of the grapevine, used in ethnic cuisine as wrappers for savoury mixtures. As the leaves are usually packed in brine, they should be well rinsed before use.

whip: to beat rapidly, incorporate air and produce expansion.

zest: thin outer layer of citrus fruits containing the aromatic citrus oil. It is usually thinly pared with a vegetable peeler, or grated with a zester or grater to separate it from the bitter white pith underneath.

weights & measures

Cooking is not an exact science: one does not require finely calibrated scales, pipettes and scientific equipment to cook, yet the conversion to metric measures in some countries and its interpretations must have intimidated many a good cook.

In the recipes weights are given for ingredients such as meats, fish, poultry and some vegetables, but in normal cooking a few ounces or grams one way or another will not affect the success of your dish.

Though recipes have been tested using the Australian Standard 250mL cup, 20mL tablespoon and 5mL teaspoon, they will work just as well with the US and Canadian 8fl oz cup, or the UK 300mL cup. We have used graduated cup measures in preference to tablespoon measures so that proportions are always the same. Where tablespoon measures have been given, these are not crucial measures, so using the smaller tablespoon of the US or UK will not affect the recipe's success. At least we all agree on the teaspoon size.

For breads, cakes and pastries, the only area which might cause concern is where eggs are used, as proportions will then vary. If working with a 250mL or 300mL cup, use large eggs (65g/$2^{1}/_{4}$oz), adding a little more liquid to the recipe for 300mL cup measures if it seems necessary. Use the medium-sized eggs (55g/2oz) with 8fl oz cup measure. A graduated set of measuring cups and spoons is recommended, the cups in particular for measuring dry ingredients. Remember to level such ingredients to ensure their accuracy.

English Measures

All measurements are similar to Australian with two exceptions: the English cup measures 300mL/10fl oz, whereas the Australian cup measure 250mL/8fl oz. The English tablespoon (the Australian dessertspoon) measures 14.8mL/$^{1}/_{2}$fl oz against the Australian tablespoon of 20mL/$^{3}/_{4}$fl oz.

American Measures

The American reputed pint is 16fl oz, a quart is equal to 32fl oz and the American gallon, 128fl oz. The Imperial measurement is 20fl oz to the pint, 40fl oz a quart and 160fl oz one gallon. The American tablespoon is equal to 14.8mL/$^{1}/_{2}$ fl oz, the teaspoon is 5mL/$^{1}/_{6}$ fl oz. The cup measure is 250mL/$8^{3}/_{4}$fl oz, the same as Australia.

Dry Measures

All the measures are level, so when you have filled a cup or spoon, level it off with the edge of a knife. The scale below is the "cook's equivalent"; it is not an exact conversion of metric to imperial measurement. To calculate the exact metric equivalent yourself, use 2.2046 lb = 1kg or 1 lb = 0.45359kg

Metric	Imperial
g = grams	oz = ounces
kg = kilograms	lb = pound
15g	$^{1}/_{2}$oz
20g	$^{2}/_{3}$oz
30g	1oz
55g	2oz
85g	3oz
115g	4oz/$^{1}/_{4}$ lb
125g	$4^{1}/_{2}$oz
145g	5oz
170g	6oz
200g	7oz
225g	8oz/$^{1}/_{2}$ lb
315g	11oz
340g	12oz
370g	13oz
400g	14oz
420g	15oz
455g	16oz
1,000g/1kg	35.3oz/2.2 lb
1.5kg	3.33 lb

Oven Temperatures

The Celsius temperatures given here are not exact; they have been rounded off and are given as a guide only. Follow the manufacturer's temperature guide, relating it to oven description given in the recipe. Remember gas ovens are hottest at the top, electric ovens at the bottom and convection-fan forced ovens are usually even throughout. We included Regulo numbers for gas cookers which may assist.

To convert °C to °F multiply °C by 9 and divide by 5 then add 32.

Oven temperatures

	C°	F°	Regular
Very slow	120	250	1
Slow	150	300	2
Moderately slow	160	325	3
Moderate	180	350	4
Moderately hot	190-200	370-400	5-6
Hot	210-220	410-440	6-7
Very hot	230	450	8
Super hot	250-290	475-500	9-10

Cake dish sizes

Metric	Imperial
15cm	6in
18cm	7in
20cm	8in
23cm	9in

Loaf dish sizes

Metric	Imperial
23 x 12cm	9 x 5in
25 x 8cm	10 x 3in
28 x 8cm	11 x 7in

Liquid measures

Metric	Imperial	Cup & Spoon
mL	fl oz	
millilitres	fluid ounce	
5mL	1/6 fl oz	1 teaspoon
20mL	2/3 fl oz	1 tablespoon
30mL	1fl oz	1 tbsp + 2tsp
55mL	2fl oz	
63mL	2 1/4 fl oz	1/4 cup
85mL	3fl oz	
115mL	4fl oz	
125mL	4 1/2 fl oz	1/2 cup
150mL	5 1/4 fl oz	
188mL	6 2/3 fl oz	3/4 cup
225mL	8fl oz	
250mL	8 3/4 fl oz	1 cup
285mL	10fl oz	
300mL	10 1/2 fl oz	
370mL	13fl oz	
400mL	14fl oz	
438mL	15 1/2 fl oz	1 3/4 cup
455mL	16fl oz	
500mL	17 1/2 fl oz	2 cups
570mL	20fl oz	
1 litre	35.3fl oz	4 cups

Length

Some of us still have trouble converting imperial length to metric. In this scale, measures have been rounded off to the easiest-to-use and most acceptable figures.

To obtain the exact metric equivalent in converting inches to centimetres, multiply inches by 2.54 whereby 1 inch equals 25.4 millimetres and 1 millimetre equals 0.03937 inches.

Metric	Imperial
mm=millimetres	in = inches
cm=centimetres	ft = feet
5mm, 0.5cm	1/4 in
10mm, 1.0cm	1/2 in
20mm, 2.0cm	3/4 in
2.5cm	1in
5cm	2in
8cm	3in
10cm	4in
12cm	5in
15cm	6in
18cm	7in
20cm	8in
23cm	9in
25cm	10in
28cm	11in
30cm	1 ft, 12in

Cup measurements

One cup is equal to the following weights.

	Metric	Imperial
Almonds, flaked	90g	3oz
Almonds, slivered, ground	125	4oz
Almonds, kernel	155g	5oz
Apples, dried, chopped	125g	4oz
Apricots, dried, chopped	190g	6oz
Breadcrumbs, packet	125g	4oz
Breadcrumbs, soft	60g	2oz
Cheese, grated	125g	4oz
Choc bits	155g	5oz
Coconut, desiccated	90g	3oz
Cornflakes	30g	1oz
Currants	155g	5oz
Flour	125g	4oz
Fruit, dried (mixed, sultanas etc)	185g	6oz
Ginger, crystallised, glace	250g	8oz
Honey, treacle, golden syrup	315g	10oz
Mixed peel	220g	7oz
Nuts, chopped	125g	4oz
Prunes, chopped	220g	7oz
Rice, cooked	155g	5oz
Rice, uncooked	220g	7oz
Rolled oats	90g	3oz
Sesame seeds	125g	4oz
Shortening (butter, margarine)	250g	8oz
Sugar, brown	155g	5oz
Sugar, granulated or caster	250g	8oz
Sugar, sifted icing	155g	5oz
Wheatgerm	60g	2oz

index

index